Reading Skills Workbook — Level 5

Table of Contents

ISBN 0-88012-677-9

Following Directions

California   Maine   Ohio
Oklahoma   Texas
New York
England   Hawaii
Georgia   Florida   Canada   Italy
Alaska
Utah   Arizona
Paris

☐ Trace the map outline in red.

☐ Put a blue **X** on any words which do not name a state.

☐ Put a green line under each state that does not end in a vowel.

☐ Put a yellow box around each state name with 4 syllables.

☐ Put a purple check by each state which ends in a vowel other than **a**.

☐ Write the three states which you have not used. Write **1,2,3** to put the words in alphabetical order.

_____   _____   _____

☐ Write the names of 5 other states which are not listed above.

1 _____   2 _____   3 _____

4 _____   5 _____

Following Directions

Follow the directions. Write.

doctor	cook	plumber

Draw a  on my head.

Draw a spoon in my hand.

Draw a bowl on the table.

I am a _____.

Draw a wrench in my hand.

Draw a plunger on the floor.

Draw water under the pipe.

I am a _____.

Draw a stethoscope around my neck.

Draw a cross on my bag.

Draw a bandage in my hand.

I am a _____.

Following Directions

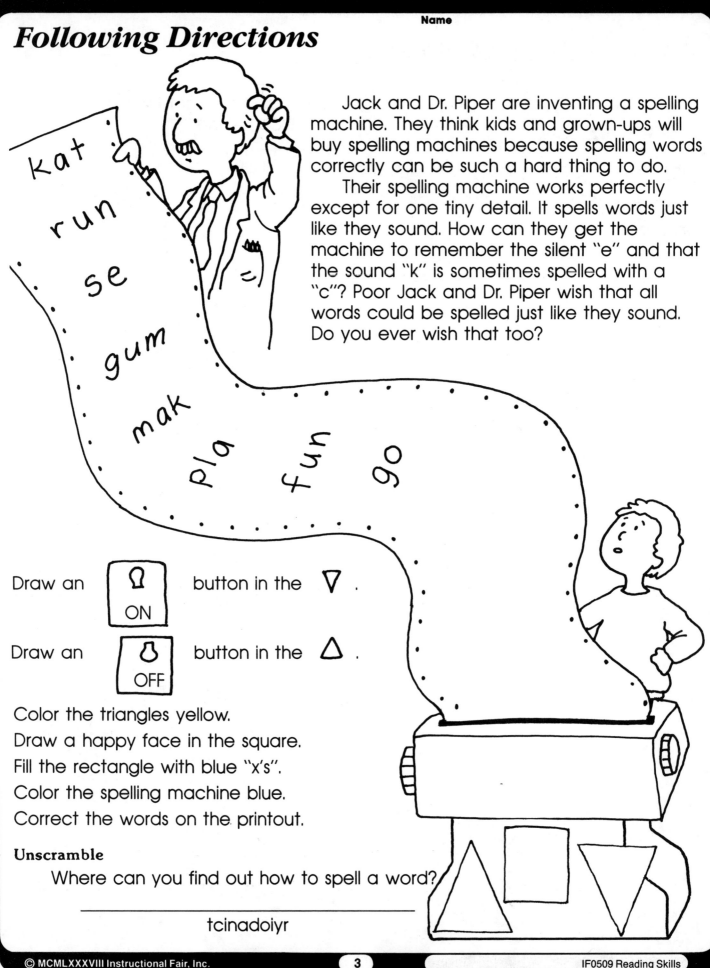

Jack and Dr. Piper are inventing a spelling machine. They think kids and grown-ups will buy spelling machines because spelling words correctly can be such a hard thing to do.

Their spelling machine works perfectly except for one tiny detail. It spells words just like they sound. How can they get the machine to remember the silent "e" and that the sound "k" is sometimes spelled with a "c"? Poor Jack and Dr. Piper wish that all words could be spelled just like they sound. Do you ever wish that too?

kat
run
se
gum
mak
pla
fun
go

Draw an [ON] button in the ▽ .

Draw an [OFF] button in the △ .

Color the triangles yellow.
Draw a happy face in the square.
Fill the rectangle with blue "x's".
Color the spelling machine blue.
Correct the words on the printout.

Unscramble

Where can you find out how to spell a word?

_____
tcinadoiyr

Following Directions

Jack and Lee are sleeping outside tonight. It's a nice night for sleeping outside. It's not too cold, and it's not too dark because the moon is full. Before they go to sleep, they talk about ghosts, monsters and UFO's and how they're not afraid of them. In the middle of the night, Jack and Lee wake up. First, they hear a loud "crash" and then a "gr-r-r" that gets louder and louder. Is it a bear? Is it a monster coming for them? What is it? Follow the directions and you will see!

Draw a tent over Jack and Lee. Color it brown.

Draw the full moon in the sky. Color it yellow.

Draw five shining stars in the sky. Color them yellow, too.

Draw an owl sitting on the branch. Color it brown.

Connect the dots by tens to see what scares Jack and Lee.

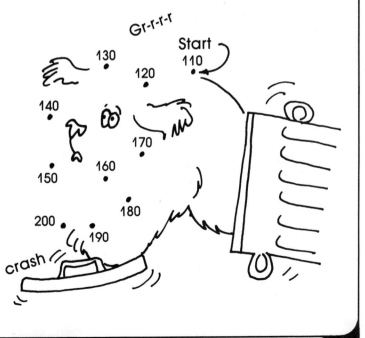

Following Directions

Read each sentence. Write each answer in the correct tag. Use the correct color.

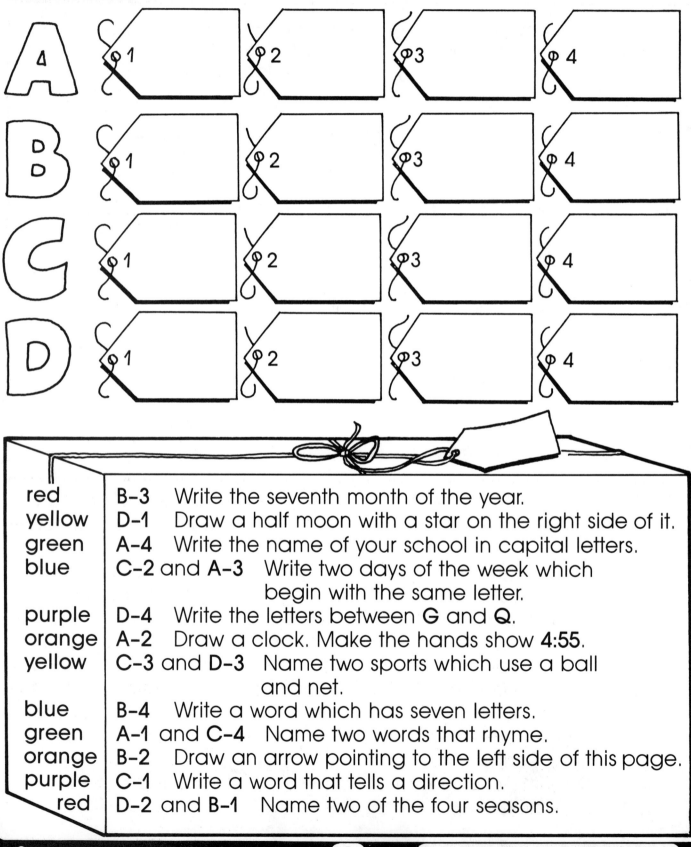

red	B-3	Write the seventh month of the year.
yellow	D-1	Draw a half moon with a star on the right side of it.
green	A-4	Write the name of your school in capital letters.
blue	C-2 and A-3	Write two days of the week which begin with the same letter.
purple	D-4	Write the letters between **G** and **Q**.
orange	A-2	Draw a clock. Make the hands show **4:55**.
yellow	C-3 and D-3	Name two sports which use a ball and net.
blue	B-4	Write a word which has seven letters.
green	A-1 and C-4	Name two words that rhyme.
orange	B-2	Draw an arrow pointing to the left side of this page.
purple	C-1	Write a word that tells a direction.
red	D-2 and B-1	Name two of the four seasons.

Following Directions

Unscramble each planet name and write it on a line.

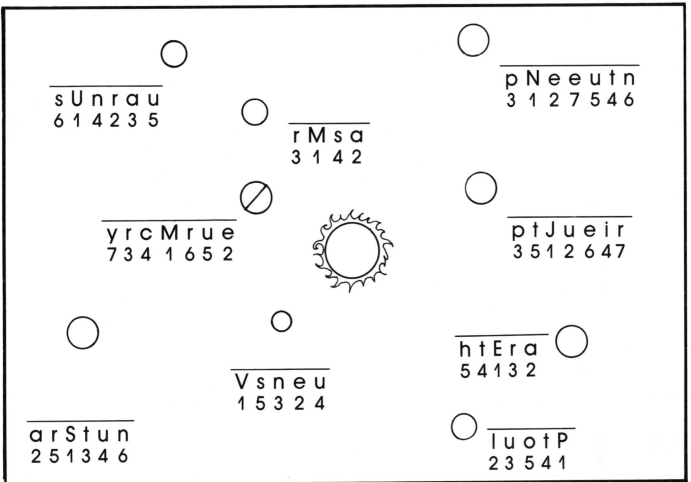

1. Pluto is the ninth planet from the sun. Write a blue nine on Pluto.
2. Mars is nicknamed the Red Planet. Use red to write the nickname
3. by the planet.
   Jupiter has sixteen moons. Make 16 yellow dots around Jupiter.
4. Uranus is almost two billion miles from Earth. The number two billion has nine zeroes. Use purple to write this number by Uranus.
5. Saturn is famous for its rings. Draw four orange rings around Saturn.
6. Earth is the third planet from the sun. Write a black three on Earth.
7. Mercury has a freezing cold side and a burning hot side. Color the side next to the sun red. Color the side away from the sun blue.
8. Venus is the nearest planet to Earth. Draw a red line between Venus and Earth.
9. Neptune is the eighth planet from the sun. Make eight green checks by Neptune.

Following Directions

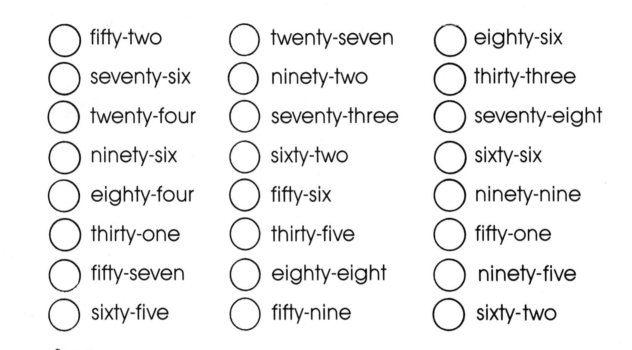

each ◯ : red —numbers between **twenty-two** and **thirty-eight**.
blue —numbers which begin with **fifty**.
green—numbers between **sixty-one** and **seventy-nine**.
purple—numbers above **eighty**.

◯ fifty-two   ◯ twenty-seven   ◯ eighty-six

◯ seventy-six   ◯ ninety-two   ◯ thirty-three

◯ twenty-four   ◯ seventy-three   ◯ seventy-eight

◯ ninety-six   ◯ sixty-two   ◯ sixty-six

◯ eighty-four   ◯ fifty-six   ◯ ninety-nine

◯ thirty-one   ◯ thirty-five   ◯ fifty-one

◯ fifty-seven   ◯ eighty-eight   ◯ ninety-five

◯ sixty-five   ◯ fifty-nine   ◯ sixty-two

the correct numerals for each number below. Use the correct colors to write the numerals:
green—numbers **above** fifty   red—numbers **below** fifty.

____ twenty-nine   ____sixty-three

____ seventy-two   ____forty-nine

____ ninety-five   ____fifty-eight

____ forty-three   ____twenty-four

____ eighty-seven   ____thirty-three

____ thirty-six   ____eighty-one

Following Directions

Jack and Ron are playing several games of tennis.

1. It is a very hot day. Draw a yellow sun in the sky above the shortest tree.
2. Use red to mark the thermometer up to **93** degrees.
3. Jack is on the right side of the net. Color his shirt yellow and his shorts blue with a green stripe.
4. Color Ron's shorts the color of Jack's stripe. Color his shirt the color of Jack's shorts.
5. Ron has just hit the ball. It is in the air, but it has not gone over the net yet. Use yellow to draw the ball.
6. Jack dropped his racket. Use brown to draw the racket.
7. Count all of the balls on the ground. Add your age to that number. Write the total in the top of the tallest tree.
8. On the tree trunk of the middle tree, write the names of three other sports which use balls.
9. Between the shortest tree and the middle tree, write three words that you can make from the letters in the word tennis.

Following Directions

Four friends have new T-shirts. Help them put a name on each.

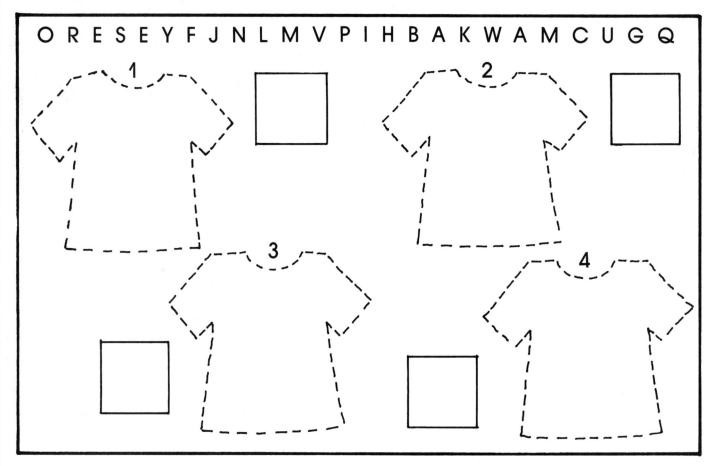

O R E S E Y F J N L M V P I H B A K W A M C U G Q

Look at the line of letters:
1. Use **red** to circle one each of these letters: A L P U
2. Use **green** to circle one each of these letters: K E M I
3. Use **yellow** to circle one each of these letters: Y A R M
4. Use **purple** to circle one each of these letters: O J E
5. Write the red circled letters in the box by shirt number **3**.
6. Write the green circled letters in the box by shirt number **1**.
7. Write the yellow circled letters in the box by shirt number **4**.
8. Write the purple circled letters in the box by shirt number **2**.
9. Unscramble the letters to make four names. Write each name on the shirt using the same color you used to circle the letters.
10. Outline each shirt this way:
   Outline Mary's shirt with the color of Joe's letters.
   Outline Paul's shirt with the color of Mike's letters.
   Outline Mike's shirt with the color of Mary's letters.
   Outline Joe's shirt with the color of Paul's letters.

Following Directions

Beth told her friends that she would wrap and tag their gifts for Tom's birthday party. But Beth seems to need your help.

1. Find the long, circular gift. Color the package purple and the bow orange with green dots.
2. Find the large, square gift. Color the package red, the ribbon blue and the bow yellow.
3. Find the gift with the plaid bow. Outline the package with green. Color the bow red.
4. Find the large, rectangular gift. Color the package yellow with red dots on it. Color the ribbon and bow red.
5. Find the large, circular package. Outline the package with purple. Color the inside orange.
6. Find tag number **2**: Write: To Tom, From Jack. Outline the tag with red.
7. Find tag number **5**: Write: To Tom, From Meg. Outline the tag with yellow.
8. Find tag number **1**: Write: To Tom, From Jason. Outline the tag with green.
9. Find tag number **3**: Write: To Tom, From Kim. Outline the tag with purple.
10. Find tag number **4**: Write: To Tom, From Ron. Outline the tag with green.

Sequencing

Look at the picture story. Read all of the sentences. Then write 1, 2, 3, or 4 by each sentence to tell the order of the story.

_____ Lee and Karen worked for several days.

_____ Karen and Lee would like a tree house.

_____ At last, they had a super tree house!

_____ They went to get some wood and the tools.

Sequencing

Put each list of things in order by numbering them from 1 to 4.

Number these items from shortest (1) to longest (4).

_____ car   _____ spoon

_____ bicycle   _____ broom

_____ skateboard   _____ telephone pole

_____ train   _____ toothpick

Number these items from softest (1) to hardest (4).

_____ cotton candy   _____ grass

_____ lollipop   _____ carpet

_____ apple   _____ pillow

_____ bread   _____ concrete

Number these items from youngest (1) to oldest (4).

_____ parent   _____ seedling

_____ baby   _____ tree

_____ toddler   _____ seed

_____ teenager   _____ sapling

Number these items from smallest (1) to largest (4).

_____ football   _____ towel

_____ tennis ball   _____ postage stamp

_____ basketball   _____ blanket

_____ ping-pong ball   _____ pot holder

Sequencing

Fill in the blank spaces with the next item in the series.

1. Saturday, Sunday, Monday, _____

2. Wednesday, Thursday, Friday, _____

3. December, January, February, _____

4. July, September, November, _____

5. Saturday, Monday, Wednesday, _____

6. December, November, October, _____

7. Thursday, Tuesday, Sunday, _____

8. April, July, October, _____

9. winter, spring, summer, _____

10. candy cane - Christmas, turkey - Thanksgiving, pumpkin - _____

11. 4th of July - fireworks, Easter - baskets, Valentine's Day - _____

12. fall - Halloween, winter - Christmas, spring - _____

Sequencing

Read each story. Then draw a line under the phrase that tells what happened before.

Bob's mother had a baby. Bob is very happy now that he has someone to play with. He is hoping that his new little brother will grow up quickly.

Before the baby came . . .

Bob went swimming.
Bob was the only child.
Bob was sick.

Jim ate his breakfast. First he had cereal, and then he ate his toast and drank his milk. Then he put on his coat and went out to play.

Before Jim ate his breakfast . . .

he was in bed sleeping.
he was in school reading.
he was chopping wood.

Jason and Kara fed the pigs and the chickens. Then they went out into the field to bring in a calf. After that they played in the hay.

Before the children could play they had to . . .

drive the tractor.
do some work.
go to school.

On Monday morning, all the children in Mrs. Becker's class came in and sat down. She told them that if they got all of their work finished on time, she had a special surprise.

Before the children got the surprise they had to . . .

wait until tomorrow.
go out for recess.
get their work done on time.

Sequencing

Read each story. Then draw a line under the phrase that tells what happened next.

Mary went to the store for Mother. She bought some clothespins, a basket and some soap. The clerk put it all in a bag. Then Mary went home.

What will mother do next?

Make some cookies.
Wash some clothes.
Go to bed.

Mike was walking down the street. He saw a little boy fall off his bike. Mike went over to help the little boy.

What might happen next?

Mike would take the little boy home.
Mike would steal the bike.
Mike would go straight to his house.

Nora was eating lunch when suddenly she smelled smoke. She turned around and saw a fire on the stove. Nora jumped up and ran to the stove.

What will Nora do next?

Eat her lunch.
Watch the fire.
Put out the fire.

The children were playing in the snow. They made a snowman and put a hat on its head. Then the sun came out.

What might happen next?

A blizzard will start.
They will go swimming.
The snowman will melt.

Sequencing

Number these sentences in order from 1 to 7 to tell a story.

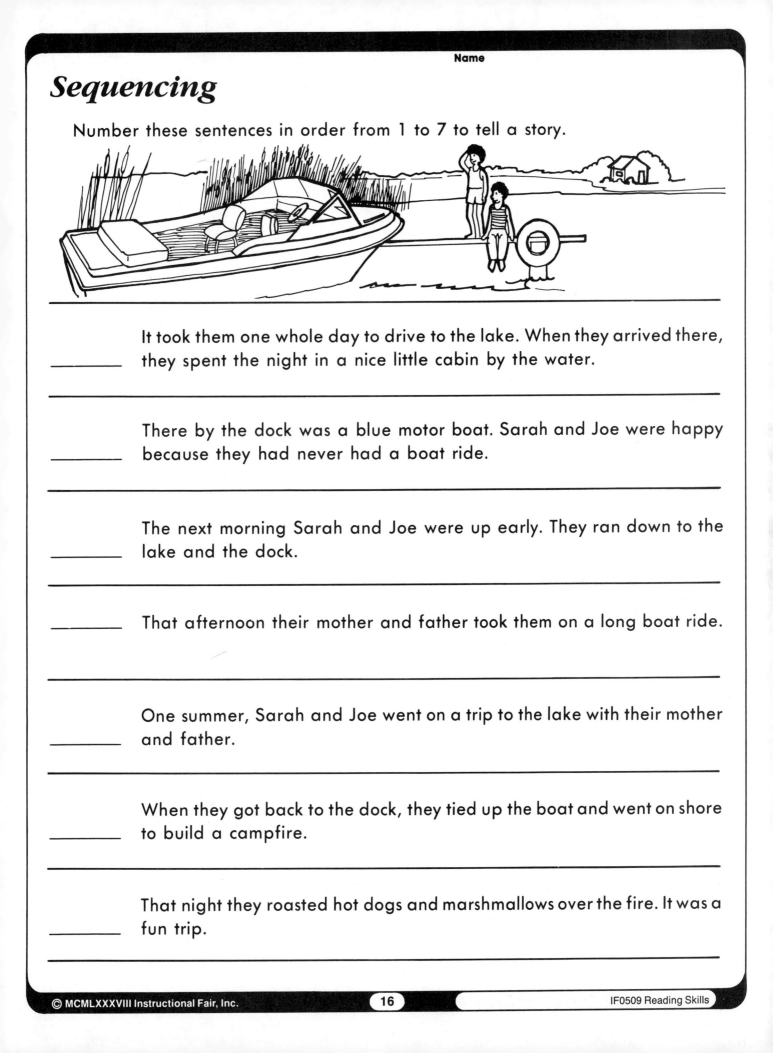

_____ It took them one whole day to drive to the lake. When they arrived there, they spent the night in a nice little cabin by the water.

_____ There by the dock was a blue motor boat. Sarah and Joe were happy because they had never had a boat ride.

_____ The next morning Sarah and Joe were up early. They ran down to the lake and the dock.

_____ That afternoon their mother and father took them on a long boat ride.

_____ One summer, Sarah and Joe went on a trip to the lake with their mother and father.

_____ When they got back to the dock, they tied up the boat and went on shore to build a campfire.

_____ That night they roasted hot dogs and marshmallows over the fire. It was a fun trip.

Sequencing

Lee's parrot Percy likes to play dead. He practices a lot and is quite good at it. When he is twenty-one, he will go to Hollywood to become a great star.

One afternoon, he gets Lee into trouble. First, he flies around Lee's room pulling out feathers. Second, he rolls around on the rug squawking and screeching. Third, he lays on the floor with his tongue hanging out and his legs pointing up.

Mom rushes into Lee's room to see what is happening. She gets mad at Lee when she thinks Percy is dead. When Mom sees that it's really a trick, she puts Percy in his cage for a week. He's grounded. He cannot leave his cage and will be totally ignored when he yells, "Percy wants a cracker!"

Write.

What will Percy do when he is twenty-one?

_____

Circle and number in 1, 2, 3 order.

☐ Percy lays on the   floor / bed   with his   ears / tongue   hanging out.

☐ Percy flies around   Mom's / Lee's   room pulling out   feathers. / hair.

☐ Percy rolls   over / around   on the rug   squawking / laughing   and screeching.

• **SOMETHING EXTRA** •

Do you know a pet that likes to do tricks? What are the tricks?

Sequencing

All of Dudley's dinner guests arrive promptly at eight except Pamela Poodle who couldn't decide what she should wear. Dudley greets them with a glass of milk and little beef bones. Then, he rings a small bell and tells all the guests, "Dinner is served."

Dudley wheels in a cart loaded with food. First, he serves salad in small wooden bowls. After the salad, he serves chicken chow mein. Some of his guests try to use chopsticks, but dogs will be dogs, so they finally give up and eat like dogs usually do. Then for dessert, each guest gets a fortune cookie with a fortune inside that Dudley promises will come true.

Write.

Why does Pamela Poodle arrive after eight o'clock?

_____

Circle in 1, 2, 3 order.

Dudley serves...

1	2	3	chicken chow mein.
1	2	3	salad.
1	2	3	fortune cookies.

Underline.

Each fortune cookie has a...
    fortune inside.
    gumdrop inside.

•SOMETHING EXTRA•

Write a fortune for Montgomery Mutt on his paper.

Sequencing

Andy sits in his highchair, quietly eating his oatmeal and toast. Mom asks Kim to keep her eye on him while she takes a hot dish over to the Sweetlys'. Kim says she will, and then she sits down at the table.

As soon as Mom leaves, Andy starts playing with his food. First, he pokes holes in his toast and holds it up to his face like a mask. Kim rolls her eyes and looks at the door. Then, he rolls his oatmeal into a ball. When he starts to throw his bowl, Kim yells, "No!" and grabs it. Then, Andy smashes some oatmeal in his face, giggling and snorting like little kids do. Kim washes his face and has to laugh, too.

Kim and Andy hear steps at the door. Andy sits in his highchair, quietly eating his oatmeal and toast.

Write.

Why does Mom ask Kim to keep her eye on Andy?

_____

Circle in 1, 2, 3, 4 order.

rolls his oatmeal into a ball.	1	2	3	4
pokes holes in his toast.	1	2	3	4
holds his toast up like a mask.	1	2	3	4
smashes oatmeal in his face.	1	2	3	4

Check.

When Mom comes back from the Sweetlys', Andy...

☐ giggles and snorts. ☐ sits quietly eating. ☐ pokes holes in his toast.

•SOMETHING EXTRA•

What are some funny things you did with your food when you were little?

Sequencing

Read the story.

Benji was a cute little brown puppy, that loved to play in the woods. He also played with Annie, the cat that lived next door, and Bobby, the dog from up the street.

Benji was always getting into trouble. If he wasn't digging in the garden, he was stealing slippers, balls, and anything else that people left around.

One day he was out in the woods. Suddenly, he saw a new friend. This new friend was black and white and very furry. He also had a big tail and two very black eyes.

Benji was very excited about this new playmate. He ran around him barking and jumping. The new friend was not very friendly. He did not like Benji at all. Suddenly, Benji was sprayed with a very bad smell. That new friend was not for him!

What was Benji's new friend? _____

Number these sentences from 1 to 5 to show when things happened in the story.

_____   Benji was sprayed with a bad smell.

_____   Benji liked to play with Annie and Bobby.

_____   Benji found a new friend in the woods.

_____   This new friend did not like Benji's jumping and barking.

_____   Benji was a cute little brown puppy.

Vocabulary

Unscramble each "noise" word. Choose the correct word for each sentence.

t i r u l s g n	o i g h n l w	i e c d h m	e k c a e r d
4 6 1 2 5 3 8 7	2 5 7 1 6 4 3	3 5 1 6 2 4	3 5 1 4 6 2 7

p p p e o d	z l d s e i z	d e c s e e c h r	a c s h r d e
1 3 4 5 2 6	3 5 7 1 6 2 4	9 4 2 1 5 8 6 7 3	3 1 4 5 2 7 6

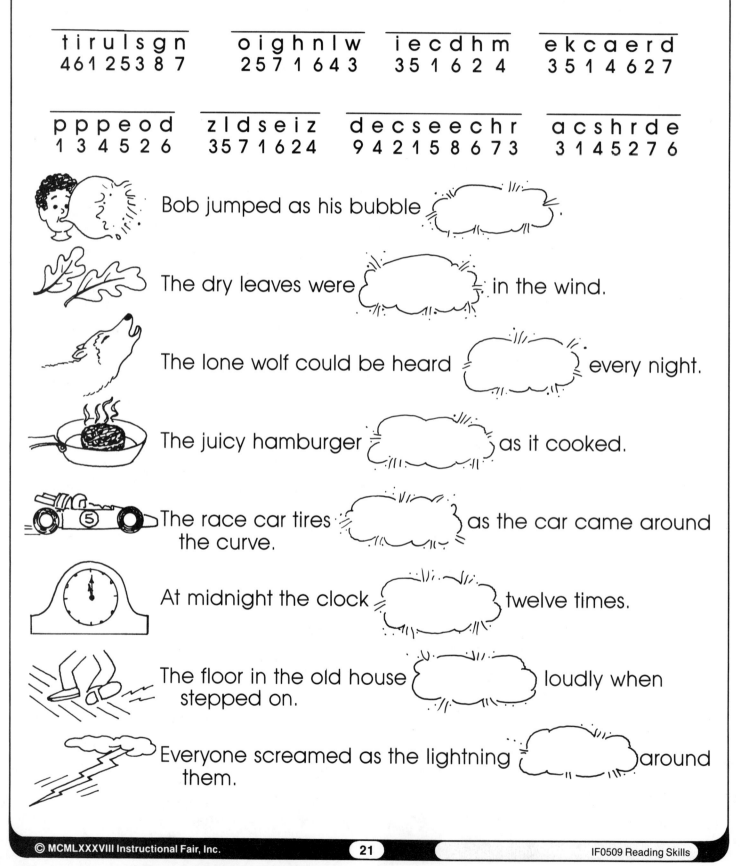

Bob jumped as his bubble _____.

The dry leaves were _____ in the wind.

The lone wolf could be heard _____ every night.

The juicy hamburger _____ as it cooked.

The race car tires _____ as the car came around the curve.

At midnight the clock _____ twelve times.

The floor in the old house _____ loudly when stepped on.

Everyone screamed as the lightning _____ around them.

Vocabulary

Unscramble each word. Draw a line to the correct definition. Write each word in the correct space in the puzzle.

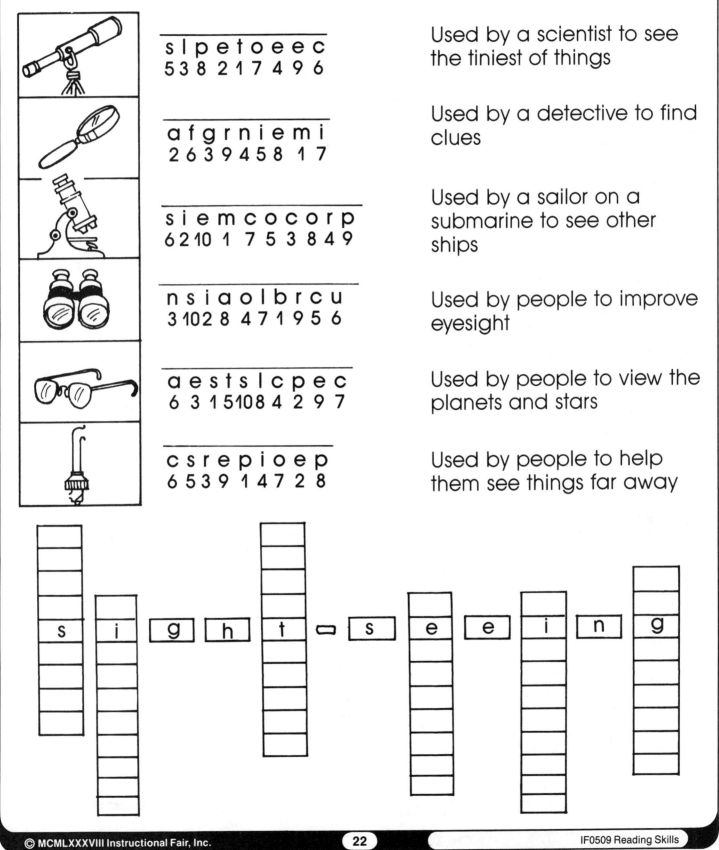

s l p e t o e e c
5 3 8 2 1 7 4 9 6

a f g r n i e m i
2 6 3 9 4 5 8 1 7

s i e m c o c o r p
6 2 10 1 7 5 3 8 4 9

n s i a o l b r c u
3 10 2 8 4 7 1 9 5 6

a e s t s l c p e c
6 3 1 5 10 8 4 2 9 7

c s r e p i o e p
6 5 3 9 1 4 7 2 8

Used by a scientist to see the tiniest of things

Used by a detective to find clues

Used by a sailor on a submarine to see other ships

Used by people to improve eyesight

Used by people to view the planets and stars

Used by people to help them see things far away

s i g h t - s e e i n g

Vocabulary

Read each note and . . .
- Use red to underline the word or words which tell **who**.
- Use blue to underline the word or words which tell **what**.
- Use yellow to underline the word or words which tell **when**.
- Use green to underline the word or words which tell **where**.

Dear Frank,
    Meet me after school at the track field to look for my lost track shoes.
                Ted

Dear Susan,
    Meet me for a movie this Saturday morning at 10:00 at the New Plaza Theater.
                Frannie

Dear Grandpa,
    Meet me at Disneyland next Saturday at 10:00 for my birthday party.
                Lee

Dear Mike,
    Meet me in two weeks to practice piano in the new band room.
                Sal

Dear Mom,
    Meet me at school this afternoon at 4:00 to give me my play costume.
                Lucy

Write a note!

Underline it too!

Dear _____,

    Meet me _____

_____

_____

_____

Vocabulary

Read each math sentence at the bottom of each page. Write the correct word to complete each sentence. Write the correct math word to name each picture.

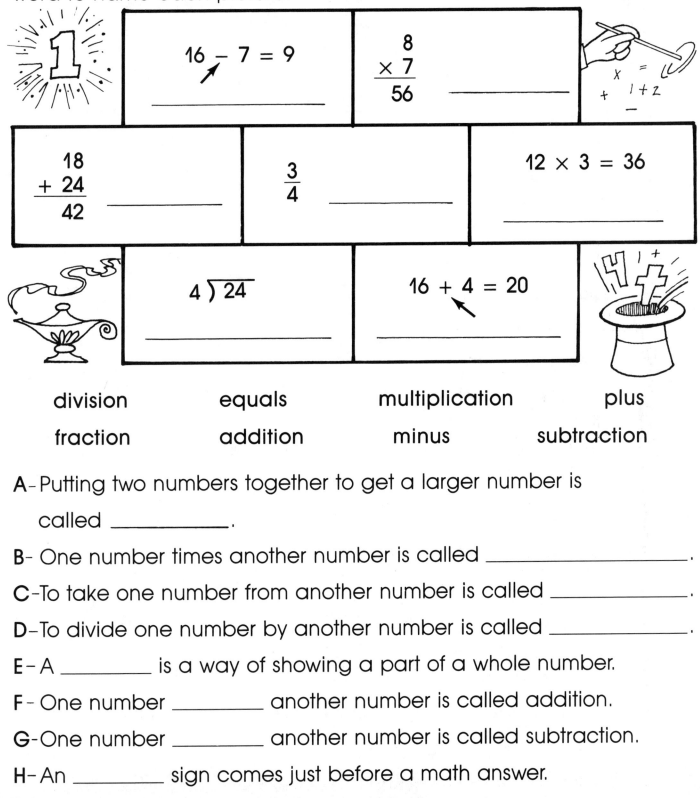

16 – 7 = 9 _____

8
× 7
56 _____

18
+ 24
42 _____

3/4 _____

12 × 3 = 36 _____

4) 24 _____

16 + 4 = 20 _____

division   equals   multiplication   plus

fraction   addition   minus   subtraction

A– Putting two numbers together to get a larger number is

called _____.

B– One number times another number is called _____.

C– To take one number from another number is called _____.

D– To divide one number by another number is called _____.

E– A _____ is a way of showing a part of a whole number.

F– One number _____ another number is called addition.

G– One number _____ another number is called subtraction.

H– An _____ sign comes just before a math answer.

Vocabulary

Circle the correct name for each picture. Write the word on the lines to complete each sentence. Write each word in the puzzle.

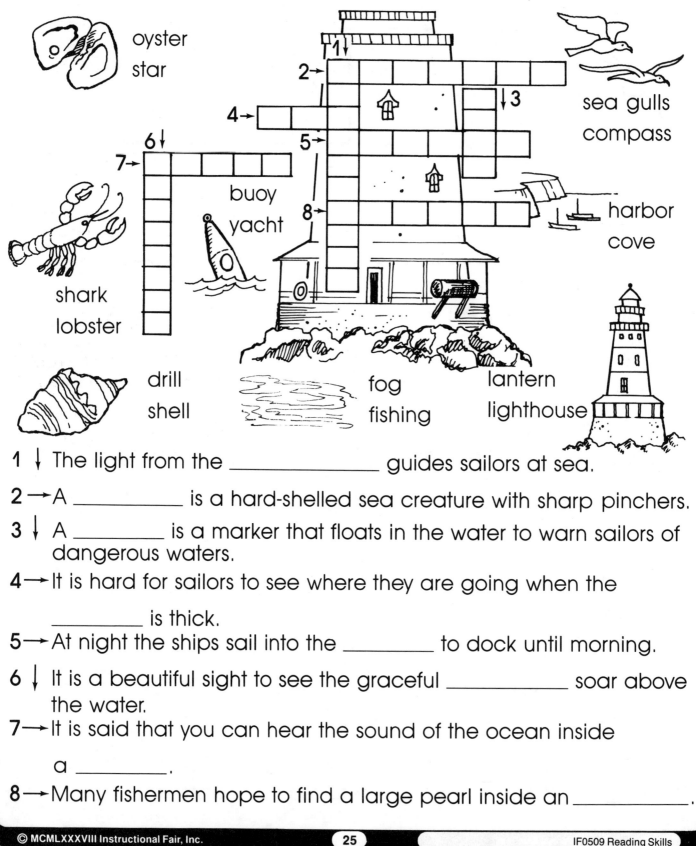

oyster
star

sea gulls
compass

buoy
yacht

harbor
cove

shark
lobster

drill
shell

fog
fishing

lantern
lighthouse

1 ↓ The light from the _____ guides sailors at sea.

2 → A _____ is a hard-shelled sea creature with sharp pinchers.

3 ↓ A _____ is a marker that floats in the water to warn sailors of dangerous waters.

4 → It is hard for sailors to see where they are going when the _____ is thick.

5 → At night the ships sail into the _____ to dock until morning.

6 ↓ It is a beautiful sight to see the graceful _____ soar above the water.

7 → It is said that you can hear the sound of the ocean inside a _____.

8 → Many fishermen hope to find a large pearl inside an _____.

Vocabulary

Trace the footprints: red - **mystery words**   yellow - **other words**

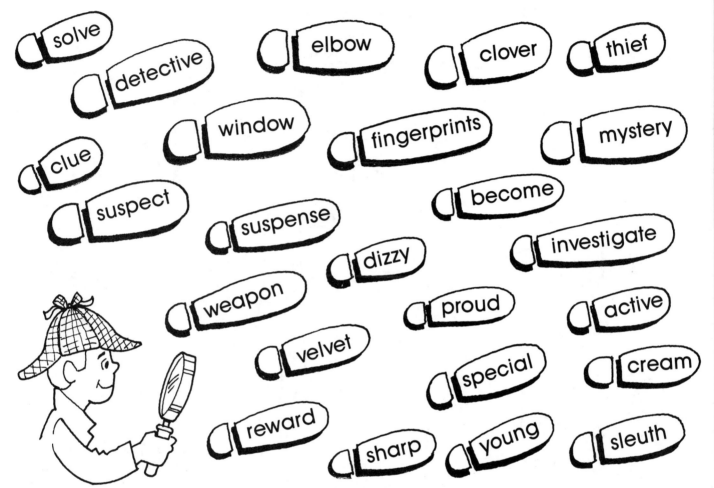

solve
detective
elbow
clover
thief
window
fingerprints
mystery
clue
suspect
become
suspense
investigate
dizzy
weapon
proud
active
velvet
special
cream
reward
sharp
young
sleuth

Write 5 of the mystery words in the footprints below. Use each in a sentence.

:_____

:_____

:_____

:_____

:_____

Vocabulary

Unscramble each word. Use the correct color to trace the line from each word to the matching part of the body. Use the same color to write each word in the correct sentence.

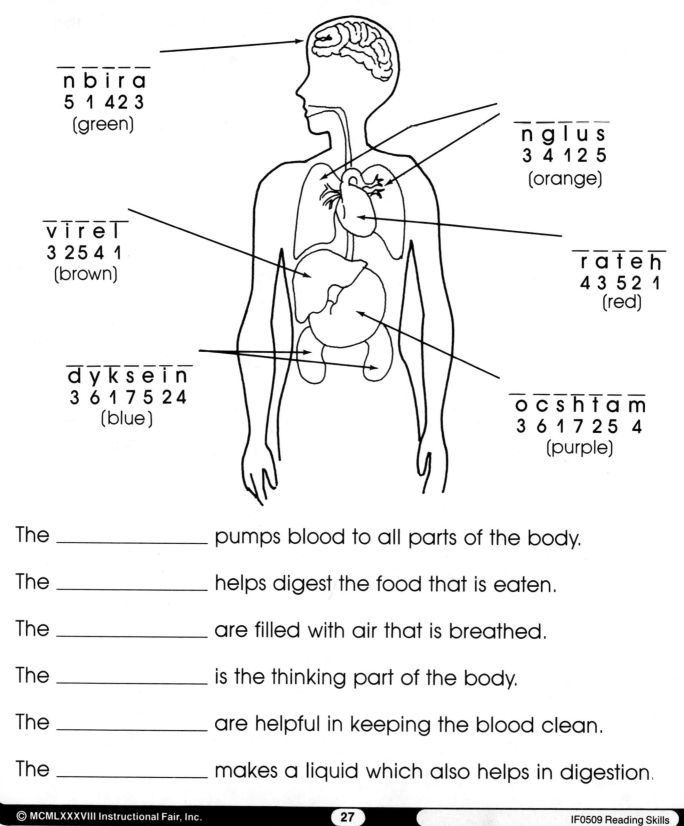

n b i r a
5 1 4 2 3
(green)

n g l u s
3 4 1 2 5
(orange)

v i r e l
3 2 5 4 1
(brown)

r a t e h
4 3 5 2 1
(red)

d y k s e i n
3 6 1 7 5 2 4
(blue)

o c s h t a m
3 6 1 7 2 5 4
(purple)

The _____ pumps blood to all parts of the body.

The _____ helps digest the food that is eaten.

The _____ are filled with air that is breathed.

The _____ is the thinking part of the body.

The _____ are helpful in keeping the blood clean.

The _____ makes a liquid which also helps in digestion.

ANSWER KEY

Reading Skills Reproducible Workbook
Level 3

This answer key has been placed in the center of this workbook so that it may be easily removed if you so desire.

The worksheet pages in this Reproducible Workbook were taken from various Instructional Fair duplicating books. To match a page from this workbook to its duplicating book source, please see the list below.

Worksheet Page Numbers in This Workbook	From Duplicating Book
1, 5-10, 21-31, 34-36, 42-46, 48-51	IF1025 Basic Reading Skills
2-4, 53, 54	IF1519 Inference, Evaluation, Following Directions
11-16, 20, 52	IF2103 Sequencing
17-19, 47	IF1513 Details, Main Idea, Sequencing
32, 33, 37-41	IF1516 Character Analysis, Prediction, Similarities & Differences

Panel 1

Following Directions

(Map of the United States with labels: red, California, Maine, Ohio, Oklahoma, New York, England, Hawaii, Texas, Georgia, Florida, Canada, Alaska, Utah, Paris, Arizona)

- ☐ Trace the map outline in red.
- ☐ Put a blue X on any words which do not name a state.
- ☐ Put a green line under each state that does not end in a vowel.
- ☐ Put a yellow box around each state name with 4 syllables.
- ☐ Put a purple check by each state which ends in a vowel other than a.
- ☐ Write the three states which you have not used. Write 1,2,3 to put the words in alphabetical order.

  1 Alaska   2 Florida   3 Georgia

- ☐ Write the names of 5 other states which are not listed above.

  1 _____ 2 _____ 3 _____

  Answers   4 _____ 5 _____
  will vary.

1

Panel 2

Following Directions

Follow the directions. Write.   doctor cook plumber

Draw a [hat] on my head.
Draw a [spoon] in my hand.
Draw a [bowl] on the table.
I am a _____

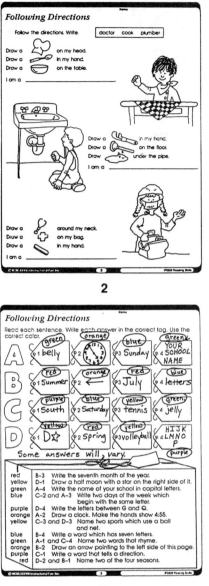

Draw a [tool] in my hand.
Draw [tool] on the floor.
Draw [tool] under the pipe.
I am a _____

Draw a [stethoscope] around my neck.
Draw a [cross] on my bag.
Draw a [thermometer] in my hand.
I am a _____

2

Panel 3

Following Directions

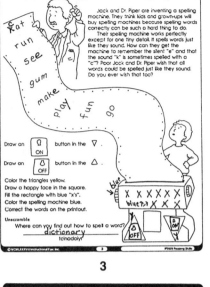

Jack and Dr. Piper are inventing a spelling machine. They think kids and grown-ups will buy spelling machines because spelling words correctly can be such a hard thing to do. Their spelling machine works perfectly except for one tiny detail. It spells words just like they sound. How can they get the machine to remember the silent "e" and that the sound "k" is sometimes spelled with a "c"? Poor Jack and Dr. Piper wish that all words could be spelled just like they sound. Do you ever wish that too?

(words: Kat, run, see, gum, make, play, fun, go)

Draw an [ON] button in the ▽.
Draw an [OFF] button in the △.

Color the triangles yellow.
Draw a happy face in the square.
Fill the rectangle with blue "x's".
Color the spelling machine blue.
Correct the words on the printout.

Unscramble
Where can you find out how to spell a word?
dictionary   tcinadoiy

3

Panel 4

Following Directions

Jack and Lee are sleeping outside tonight. It's a nice night for sleeping outside. It's not too cold, and it's not too dark because the moon is full. Before they go to sleep, they talk about ghosts, monsters and UFO's and how they're not afraid of them. In the middle of the night, Jack and Lee woke up. First, they hear a loud "crash" and then a "light-r" that gets louder and louder. Is it a bear? Is it a monster coming for them? What is it? Follow the directions and you will see!

Draw a tent over Jack and Lee. Color it brown.

Draw the full moon in the sky. Color it yellow.

Draw five shining stars in the sky. Color them yellow, too.

Draw an owl sitting on the branch. Color it brown.

Connect the dots by tens to see what scared Jack and Lee.

4

Panel 5

Following Directions

Read each sentence. Write each answer in the correct tag. Use the correct color.

(grid A, B, C, D with colored tags: green belly, orange clock, blue Sunday, green YOUR SCHOOL NAME / red Summer, orange, red July, blue letters / purple South, blue Saturday, yellow tennis, green jelly / yellow D☆, red Spring, yellow volleyball, HIJK LMNO P, purple)

Some answers will vary.

red	B-3	Write the seventh month of the year.
yellow	D-1	Draw a half moon with a star on the right side of it.
green	A-4	Write the name of your school in capital letters.
blue	C-2 and A-3	Write two days of the week which begin with the same letter.
purple	D-4	Write the letters between G and Q.
orange	A-2	Draw a clock. Make the hands show 4:55.
yellow	C-3 and D-3	Name two sports which use a ball and net.
blue	B-4	Write a word which has seven letters.
green	A-1 and C-4	Name two words that rhyme.
orange	B-2	Draw an arrow pointing to the left side of this page.
purple	A-1	Write a word that tells a direction.
red	D-2 and B-1	Name two of the four seasons.

5

Panel 6

Following Directions

Unscramble each planet name and write it on a line.

2,000,000,000

Uranus   sUnrau   614235
Red Planet Mars   rMsa   3142
Neptune   pNeeutn   3127546
Mercury   yrcMrue   7341652
Jupiter   ptJueir   3512647
Earth   hEtrc   54132
Venus   Vsneu   15324
Saturn   arStun   251346
Pluto   luotP

1. Pluto is the ninth planet from the sun. Write a blue nine on Pluto.
2. Mars is nicknamed the Red Planet. Use red to write the nickname by the planet.
   Jupiter has sixteen moons. Make 16 yellow dots around Jupiter.
4. Uranus is almost two billion miles from Earth. The number two billion has nine zeroes. Use purple to write this number by Uranus.
5. Saturn is famous for its rings. Draw four orange rings around Saturn.
6. Earth is the third planet from the sun. Write a black three on Earth.
7. Mercury has a freezing cold side and a burning hot side. Color the side next to the sun red. Color the side away from the sun blue.
8. Venus is the nearest planet to Earth. Draw a red line between Venus and Earth.
9. Neptune is the eighth planet from the sun. Make eight green checks by Neptune.

6

Panel 7

Following Directions

Color each ○: red — numbers between twenty-two and thirty-eight.
blue — numbers which begin with fifty.
green — numbers between sixty-one and seventy-nine.
purple — numbers above eighty.

- (b) fifty-two
- (g) seventy-six
- (r) twenty-four
- (p) ninety-six
- (p) eighty-four
- (r) thirty-one
- (b) fifty-seven
- (g) sixty-five
- (r) twenty-seven
- (g) ninety-two
- (g) seventy-three
- (b) sixty-two
- (r) thirty-five
- (p) eighty-eight
- (b) fifty-nine
- (p) eighty-six
- (r) thirty-three
- (g) seventy-eight
- (b) fifty-six
- (g) ninety-nine
- (b) fifty-one
- (p) ninety-five
- (g) sixty-two

Write the correct numerals for each number below. Use the correct colors to write the numerals:
green — numbers above fifty   red — numbers below fifty

- (y) 29 twenty-nine
- (y) 72 seventy-two
- (y) 95 ninety-five
- (y) 43 forty-three
- (y) 87 eighty-seven
- (y) 36 thirty-six
- (g) 63 sixty-three
- (y) 49 forty-nine
- (g) 58 fifty-eight
- (y) 24 twenty-four
- (y) 33 thirty-three
- (g) 81 eighty-one

7

Panel 8

Following Directions

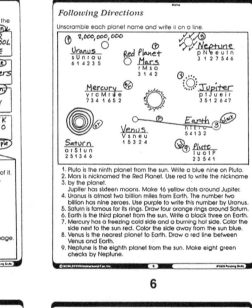

Some answers will vary.

ten in set — will vary

Jack and Ron are playing several games of tennis.

1. It is a very hot day. Draw a yellow sun in the sky above the shortest tree.
2. Use red to mark the thermometer up to 93 degrees.
3. Jack is on the right side of the net. Color his shirt yellow and his shorts blue with a green stripe.
4. Color Ron's shorts the color of Jack's stripe. Color his shirt the color of Jack's shorts.
5. Ron has just hit the ball. It is in the air, but it has not gone over the net yet. Use yellow to draw the ball.
6. Jack dropped his racket. Use brown to draw the racket.
7. Count all of the balls on the ground. Add your age to that number. Write the total in the top of the tallest tree.
8. On the tree trunk of the middle tree, write the names of three other sports which use balls.
9. Between the shortest tree and the middle tree, write three words that you can make from the letters in the word tennis.

8

Panel 9

Following Directions

Four friends have new T-shirts. Help them put a name on each.

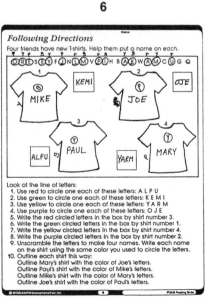

(letters row: O R E S E Y F N D M V P U H B A K W A M C U G Q)

Shirts: MIKE, KEMI, JOE, OJE, ALPU, PAUL, YARM, MARY

Look at the line of letters:
1. Use red to circle one each of these letters: A L P U
2. Use green to circle one each of these letters: K E M I
3. Use yellow to circle one each of these letters: Y A R M
4. Use purple to circle one each of these letters: O J E
5. Write the red circled letters in the box by shirt number 3.
6. Write the green circled letters in the box by shirt number 1.
7. Write the yellow circled letters in the box by shirt number 4.
8. Write the purple circled letters in the box by shirt number 2.
9. Unscramble the letters to make four names. Write each name on the shirt using the same color you used to circle the letters.
10. Outline each shirt this way:
    Outline Mary's shirt with the color of Joe's letters.
    Outline Paul's shirt with the color of Mike's letters.
    Outline Mike's shirt with the color of Mary's letters.
    Outline Joe's shirt with the color of Paul's letters.

9

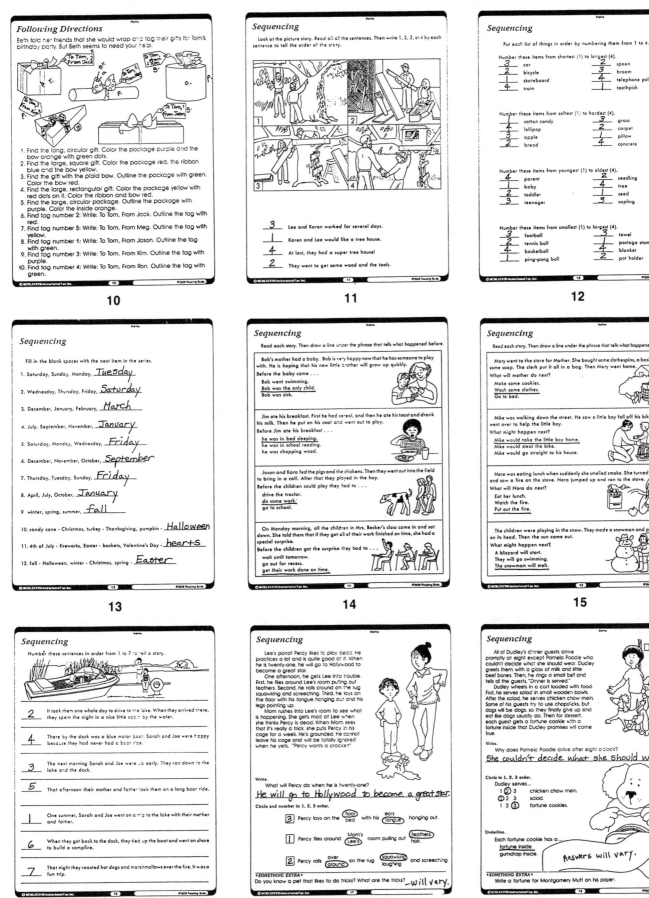

Page 10 — Following Directions

Beth told her friends that she would wrap and tag their gifts for Tom's birthday party. But Beth seems to need your help.

1. Find the long, circular gift. Color the package purple and the bow orange with green dots.
2. Find the large, square gift. Color the package red, the ribbon blue and the bow yellow.
3. Find the gift with the plaid bow. Outline the package with green. Color the bow red.
4. Find the large, rectangular gift. Color the package yellow with red dots on it. Color the ribbon and bow red.
5. Find the large, circular package. Outline the package with purple. Color the inside orange.
6. Find tag number 2: Write: To Tom, From Jack. Outline the tag with red.
7. Find tag number 5: Write: To Tom, From Meg. Outline the tag with yellow.
8. Find tag number 1: Write: To Tom, From Jason. Outline the tag with green.
9. Find tag number 3: Write: To Tom, From Kim. Outline the tag with purple.
10. Find tag number 4: Write: To Tom, From Ron. Outline the tag with green.

10

Page 11 — Sequencing

Look at the picture story. Read all of the sentences. Then write 1, 2, 3, or 4 by each sentence to tell the order of the story.

3 Lee and Karen worked for several days.

1 Karen and Lee would like a tree house.

4 At last, they had a super tree house!

2 They went to get some wood and the tools.

11

Page 12 — Sequencing

Put each list of things in order by numbering them from 1 to 4.

Number these items from shortest (1) to longest (4).

3	car		2	spoon
2	bicycle		3	broom
1	skateboard		4	telephone pole
4	train		1	toothpick

Number these items from softest (1) to hardest (4).

1	cotton candy		3	grass
4	lollipop		2	carpet
3	apple		1	pillow
2	bread		4	concrete

Number these items from youngest (1) to oldest (4).

4	parent		1	seedling
1	baby		4	tree
2	toddler		2	seed
3	teenager		3	sapling

Number these items from smallest (1) to largest (4).

3	football		3	towel
2	tennis ball		1	postage stamp
4	basketball		4	blanket
1	ping-pong ball		2	pot holder

12

Page 13 — Sequencing

Fill in the blank spaces with the next item in the series.

1. Saturday, Sunday, Monday, __Tuesday__
2. Wednesday, Thursday, Friday, __Saturday__
3. December, January, February, __March__
4. July, September, November, __January__
5. Saturday, Monday, Wednesday, __Friday__
6. December, November, October, __September__
7. Thursday, Tuesday, Sunday, __Friday__
8. April, July, October, __January__
9. winter, spring, summer, __fall__
10. candy cane - Christmas, turkey - Thanksgiving, pumpkin - __Halloween__
11. 4th of July - fireworks, Easter - baskets, Valentine's Day - __hearts__
12. fall - Halloween, winter - Christmas, spring - __Easter__

13

Page 14 — Sequencing

Read each story. Then draw a line under the phrase that tells what happened before.

Bob's mother had a baby. Bob is very happy now that he has someone to play with. He is hoping that his new little brother will grow up quickly.
Before the baby came . . .
Bob went swimming.
__Bob was the only child.__
Bob was sick.

Jim ate his breakfast. First he had cereal, and then he ate his toast and drank his milk. Then he put on his coat and went out to play.
Before Jim ate his breakfast . . .
__he was in bed sleeping.__
he was in school reading.
he was chopping wood.

Jason and Kara fed the pigs and the chickens. Then they went out into the field to bring in a calf. After that they played in the hay.
Before the children could play they had to . . .
drive the tractor.
__do some work.__
go to school.

On Monday morning, all the children in Mrs. Becker's class came in and sat down. She told them that if they got all of their work finished on time, she had a special surprise.
Before the children got the surprise they had to . . .
wait until tomorrow.
go out for recess.
__get their work done on time.__

14

Page 15 — Sequencing

Read each story. Then draw a line under the phrase that tells what happened next.

Mary went to the store for Mother. She bought some clothespins, a basket and some soap. The clerk put it all in a bag. Then Mary went home.
What will mother do next?
Make some cookies.
__Wash some clothes.__
Go to bed.

Mike was walking down the street. He saw a little boy fall off his bike. Mike went over to help the little boy.
What might happen next?
__Mike would take the little boy home.__
Mike would steal the bike.
Mike would go straight to his house.

Nora was eating lunch when suddenly she smelled smoke. She turned around and saw a fire on the stove. Nora jumped up and ran to the stove.
What will Nora do next?
Eat her lunch.
Watch the fire.
__Put out the fire.__

The children were playing in the snow. They made a snowman and put a hat on its head. Then the sun came out.
What might happen next?
A blizzard will start.
They will go swimming.
__The snowman will melt.__

15

Page 16 — Sequencing

Number these sentences in order from 1 to 7 to tell a story.

2 It took them one whole day to drive to the lake. When they arrived there, they spent the night in a nice little cabin by the water.

4 There by the dock was a blue motor boat. Sarah and Joe were happy because they had never had a boat ride.

3 The next morning Sarah and Joe were up early. They ran down to the lake and the dock.

5 That afternoon their mother and father took them on a long boat ride.

1 One summer, Sarah and Joe went on a trip to the lake with their mother and father.

6 When they got back to the dock, they tied up the boat and went on shore to build a campfire.

7 That night they roasted hot dogs and marshmallows over the fire. It was a fun trip.

16

Page 17 — Sequencing

Lee's parrot Percy likes to play dead. He practices a lot and is quite good at it. When he is twenty-one, he will go to Hollywood to become a great star.

One afternoon, he gets Lee into trouble. First, he flies around Lee's room pulling out feathers. Second, he rolls around on the rug squawking and screeching. Third, he lays on the floor with his tongue hanging out and his legs pointing up.

Mom rushes into Lee's room to see what is happening. She gets mad at Lee when she thinks Percy is dead. When Mom sees that it's really a trick, she puts Percy in his cage for a week. He's grounded. He cannot leave his cage and will be totally ignored when he yells, "Percy wants a cracker!"

Write:
What will Percy do when he is twenty-one?
__He will go to Hollywood to become a great star.__

Circle and number in 1, 2, 3 order.

3 Percy lays on the (floor) bed with his ears (tongue) hanging out.

1 Percy flies around (Lee's) Mom's room pulling out (feathers) hair.

2 Percy rolls (over) (around) on the rug (squawking) laughing and screeching.

SOMETHING EXTRA
Do you know a pet that likes to do tricks? What are the tricks? __will vary.__

17

Page 18 — Sequencing

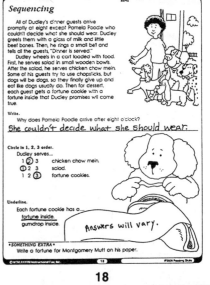

All of Dudley's dinner guests arrive promptly at eight except Pamela Poodle who couldn't decide what she should wear. Dudley greets them with a glass of milk and little beef bones. Then, he rings a small bell and tells all the guests, "Dinner is served."

Dudley wheels in a cart loaded with food. First, he serves salad in small wooden bowls. After the salad, he serves chicken chow mein. Some of his guests try to use chopsticks, but dogs will be dogs, so they finally give up and eat like dogs usually do. Then for dessert, each guest gets a fortune cookie with a fortune inside that Dudley promises will come true.

Write:
Why does Pamela Poodle arrive after eight o'clock?
__She couldn't decide what she should wear.__

Circle in 1, 2, 3 order.
Dudley serves...
1 (2) 3 chicken chow mein.
(1) 2 3 salad.
1 2 (3) fortune cookies.

Underline:
Each fortune cookie has a...
__fortune inside.__
gumdrop inside.

SOMETHING EXTRA
Write a fortune for Montgomery Mutt on his paper.

__Answers will vary.__

18

Page 19

Sequencing

Andy sits in his highchair, quietly eating his oatmeal and toast. Mom asks Kim to keep her eye on him while she takes a hot dish over to the Sweetlys'. Kim says she will, and then she sits down at the table.

As soon as Mom leaves, Andy starts playing with his food. First, he pokes holes in his toast and holds it up to his face like a mask. Kim rolls her eyes and looks at the door. Then, he rolls his oatmeal into a ball. When he starts to throw his bowl, Kim yells, "No!" and grabs it. Then, Andy smashes some oatmeal in his face, giggling and snorting like little kids do. Kim washes his face and has to laugh, too.

Kim and Andy hear steps at the door. Andy sits in his highchair, quietly eating his oatmeal and toast.

Write:
Why does Mom ask Kim to keep her eye on Andy?

She's taking a hot dish over to the Sweetlys'

Circle in 1, 2, 3, 4 order.

	1	2	3	4
rolls his oatmeal into a ball.	1	2	③	4
pokes holes in his toast.	①	2	3	4
holds his toast up like a mask.	1	②	3	4
smashes oatmeal in his face.	1	2	3	④

Check.
When Mom comes back from the Sweetlys', Andy...
- [ ] giggles and snorts. [✓] sits quietly eating. [ ] pokes holes in his toast.

SOMETHING EXTRA
What are some funny things you did with your food when you were little?
— will vary.

Page 20

Sequencing

Read the story.

Benji was a cute little brown puppy, that loved to play in the woods. He also played with Annie, the cat that lived next door, and Bobby, the dog from up the street.

Benji was always getting into trouble. If he wasn't digging in the garden, he was stealing slippers, balls, and anything else that people left around.

One day he was out in the woods. Suddenly, he saw a new friend. This new friend was black and white and very furry. He also had a big tail and two very black eyes.

Benji was very excited about this new playmate. He ran around him barking and jumping. The new friend was not very friendly. He did not like Benji at all. Suddenly, Benji was sprayed with a very bad smell. That new friend was not for him!

What was Benji's new friend? **skunk**

Number these sentences from 1 to 5 to show when things happened in the story.

5 Benji was sprayed with a bad smell.
2 Benji liked to play with Annie and Bobby.
3 Benji found a new friend in the woods.
4 This new friend did not like Benji's jumping and barking.
1 Benji was a cute little brown puppy.

Page 21

Vocabulary

Unscramble each "noise" word. Choose the correct word for each sentence.

rustling	howling	chimed	creaked
tirulsgn	olghnlw	iecdhm	ekcaerd
4 6 1 2 5 3 8 7	2 5 7 1 6 4 3	3 5 1 6 2 4	3 5 1 4 6 2 7

popped	sizzled	screeched	crashed
plpbleod	zldseiz	decseechr	acshrde
1 3 4 5 7 6 2	3 5 7 1 6 2 4	9 4 2 1 5 8 6 7 3	3 1 4 5 2 7 6

Bob jumped as his bubble **popped**.

The dry leaves were **rustling** in the wind.

The lone wolf could be heard **howling** every night.

The juicy hamburger **sizzled** as it cooked.

The race car tires **screeched** as the car came around the curve.

At midnight the clock **chimed** twelve times.

The floor in the old house **creaked** loudly when stepped on.

Everyone screamed as the lightning **crashed** around them.

Page 22

Vocabulary

Unscramble each word. Draw a line to the correct definition. Write each word in the correct space in the puzzle.

word	scramble	
telescope	sipetobec	5 3 8 2 1 7 4 9 6
magnifier	afgfniemi	2 6 3 9 4 5 8 1 7
microscope	siemcodorp	6 2 10 1 7 5 3 8 4 9
binoculars	nsiaolbrcu	3 10 2 8 4 7 1 9 5 6
spectacles	aestslcpec	6 3 1 5 10 8 4 2 9 7
periscope	c'srepidep	6 5 3 9 1 4 7 2 8

Definitions:
- Used by a scientist to see the tiniest of things
- Used by a detective to find clues
- Used by a sailor on a submarine to see other ships
- Used by people to improve eyesight
- Used by people to view the planets and stars
- Used by people to help them see things far away

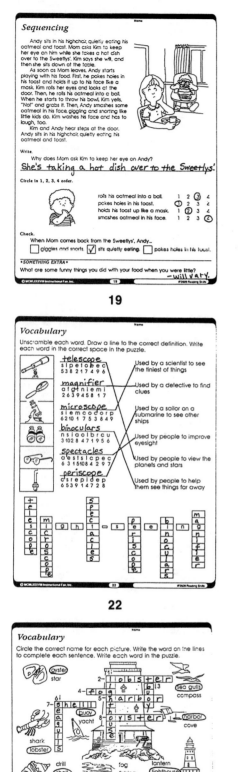

Page 23

Vocabulary

Read each note and . . .
- Use red to underline the word or words which tell who.
- Use blue to underline the word or words which tell what.
- Use yellow to underline the word or words which tell when.
- Use green to underline the word or words which tell where.

Dear Frank,
Meet me after school at the track field to look for my track shoes.
Ted

Dear Susan,
Meet me for a movie this Saturday morning at 10:00 at the New Plaza Theater.
Frannie

Dear Grandpa,
Meet me at Disneyland next Saturday at 10:00 for my birthday party.
Lee

Dear Mike,
Meet me in two weeks to practice piano in the new band room.
Sal

Dear Mom,
Meet me at school this after- noon at 4:00 to give me my play costume.
Lucy

Underline it too!
Write a note!
Dear ____,
Meet me ____

Page 24

Vocabulary

Read each math sentence at the bottom of each page. Write the correct word to complete each sentence. Write the correct math word to name each picture.

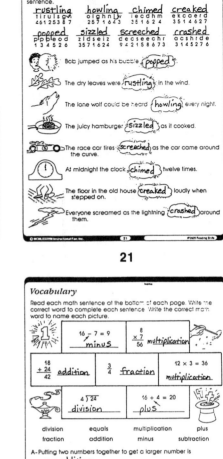

16 − 7 = 9 minus	8 ×7 56 multiplication
18 +24 42 addition	3/4 fraction	12 × 3 = 36 multiplication

4)24 division	16 ÷ 4 = 20 plus

Word bank:
division   equals   multiplication   plus
fraction   addition   minus   subtraction

A- Putting two numbers together to get a larger number is called **addition**.
B- One number times another number is called **multiplication**.
C- To take one number from another number is called **subtraction**.
D- To divide one number by another number is called **division**.
E- A **fraction** is a way of showing a part of a whole number.
F- One number **plus** another number is called addition.
G- One number **minus** another number is called subtraction.
H- An **equals** sign comes just before a math answer.

Page 25

Vocabulary

Circle the correct name for each picture. Write the word on the lines to complete each sentence. Write each word in the puzzle.

oyster / star
sea gull / compass
fog / buoy / yacht
harbor / cove
shark / lobster
drill / shell
fog / fishing
lantern / lighthouse

Puzzle: lobster, fog, harbor, shell, buoy, oyster

1 — The light from the **lighthouse** guides sailors at sea.
2 — A **lobster** is a hard-shelled sea creature with sharp pinchers.
3 — A **buoy** is a marker that floats in the water to warn sailors of dangerous waters.
4 — It is hard for sailors to see where they are going when the **fog** is thick.
5 — At night the ships sail into the **harbor** to dock until morning.
6 — It is a beautiful sight to see the graceful **sea gulls** soar above the water.
7 — It is said that you can hear the sound of the ocean inside a **shell**.
8 — Many fishermen hope to find a large pearl inside an **oyster**.

Page 26

Vocabulary

Trace the footprints: red - mystery words   yellow - other words

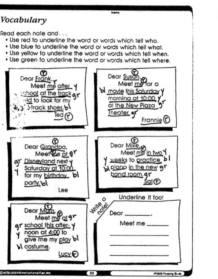

solve, detective, clue, suspect, suspense, weapon, velvet, reward, sharp, elbow, window, fingerprints, dizzy, proud, special, young, clover, become, investigate, active, cream, sleuth, thief, mystery

Write 5 of the mystery words in the footprints below. Use each in a sentence.

Answers will vary.

Page 27

Vocabulary

Unscramble each word. Use the correct color to trace the line from each word to the matching part of the body. Use the same color to write each word in the correct sentence.

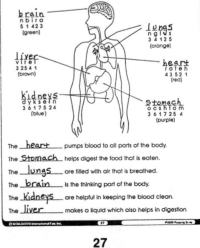

brain nbira 5 1 4 2 3 (green)	**lungs** nglus 3 4 1 2 5 (orange)
liver vlrel 3 2 5 4 1 (brown)	**heart** rateh 4 3 5 2 1 (red)
kidneys dykseln 3 6 1 7 5 2 4 (blue)	**stomach** ocshtom 3 6 1 7 2 5 4 (purple)

The **heart** pumps blood to all parts of the body.
The **stomach** helps digest the food that is eaten.
The **lungs** are filled with air that is breathed.
The **brain** is the thinking part of the body.
The **kidneys** are helpful in keeping the blood clean.
The **liver** makes a liquid which also helps in digestion.

Page 28

Vocabulary

Read each sentence. Choose the correct word to complete each sentence. Color each puzzle space the correct color.

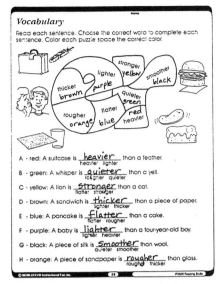

stronger yellow / lighter / smoother black / thicker brown / purple / quieter green / flatter / rougher orange / flatter blue / red heavier

A - red: A suitcase is **heavier** than a feather.
(heavier / lighter)

B - green: A whisper is **quieter** than a yell.
(rougher / quieter)

C - yellow: A lion is **stronger** than a cat.
(flatter / stronger)

D - brown: A sandwich is **thicker** than a piece of paper.
(lighter / thicker)

E - blue: A pancake is **flatter** than a cake.
(flatter / rougher)

F - purple: A baby is **lighter** than a four-year-old boy.
(lighter / heavier)

G - black: A piece of silk is **smoother** than wool.
(quieter / smoother)

H - orange: A piece of sandpaper is **rougher** than glass.
(rougher / thicker)

28

Page 29

Vocabulary

All around town are sights that you might see each day. But have you ever tried to describe them? Look at each picture. Think of four words to describe each picture. Write the words on the lines.

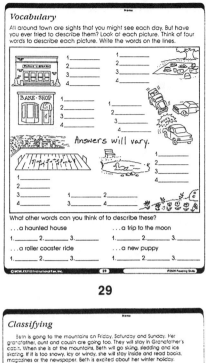

Answers will vary.

What other words can you think of to describe these?

...a haunted house
1. ___ 2. ___ 3. ___

...a roller coaster ride
1. ___ 2. ___ 3. ___

...a trip to the moon
1. ___ 2. ___ 3. ___

...a new puppy
1. ___ 2. ___ 3. ___

29

Page 30

Vocabulary

Unscramble each word to complete the sentence. The first letter is circled. Color each space the correct color.

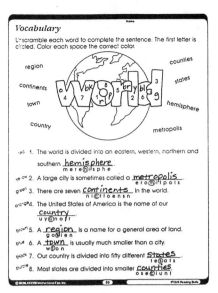

region   counties
continents   states
town   hemisphere
country   metropolis

1. The world is divided into an eastern, western, northern and southern **hemisphere**. (merehisphe)

2. A large city is sometimes called a **metropolis**. (eromitpols)

3. There are seven **continents** in the world. (nictloensn)

4. The United States of America is the name of our **country**. (uycnofr)

5. A **region** is a name for a general area of land. (goein)

6. A **town** is usually much smaller than a city. (wtion)

7. Our country is divided into fifty different **states**. (tegats)

8. Most states are divided into smaller **counties**. (oseciunt)

30

Page 31

Classifying

Answers will vary.

1. Name 4 things that will: **float**
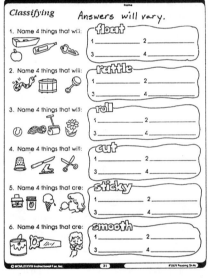
1. ___ 2. ___ 3. ___ 4. ___

2. Name 4 things that will: **rattle**
1. ___ 2. ___ 3. ___ 4. ___

3. Name 4 things that will: **roll**
1. ___ 2. ___ 3. ___ 4. ___

4. Name 4 things that will: **cut**
1. ___ 2. ___ 3. ___ 4. ___

5. Name 4 things that are: **sticky**
1. ___ 2. ___ 3. ___ 4. ___

6. Name 4 things that are: **smooth**
1. ___ 2. ___ 3. ___ 4. ___

31

Page 32

Classifying

Beth is going to the mountains on Friday, Saturday and Sunday. Her grandfather, aunt and cousin are going too. They will stay in Grandfather's cabin. When she is at the mountains, Beth will go skiing, sledding and ice skating. If it is too snowy, icy or windy, she will stay inside and read books, magazines or the newspaper. Beth is excited about her winter holiday.

Check.
Beth is going to the...
☐ beach.
☑ mountains.

Circle.
She feels...
brave.
(excited.)

Underline.
They will stay in Grandpa's...
motel.
lodge.
<u>cabin.</u>

Write.

Day Words	Family Words	Sports Words
Friday	grandfather	skiing
Saturday	aunt	sledding
Sunday	cousin	ice skating

Weather Words	Things to Read
snowy	books
icy	magazines
windy	newspaper

32

Page 33

Classifying

Write each word under its correct heading. Check each word off as you write.

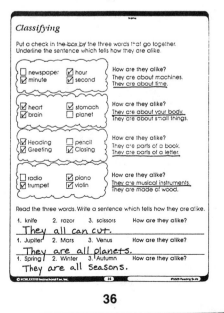

early✓   little✓   planet✓   huge✓   policeman✓
tiny✓   month✓   throw✓   fireman✓   beach✓
week✓   city✓   mailman✓   soon✓   eat✓
teacher✓   jump✓   late✓   library✓   skip✓
drive✓   baker✓   skinny✓   large✓   farm✓

Action Words	Job Words	Size Words
drive	teacher	tiny
jump	baker	little
throw	mailman	skinny
eat	fireman	huge
skip	policeman	large

Time Words	Place Words	Write the place words in alphabetical order.
early	city	beach
week	planet	city
month	library	farm
late	beach	library
soon	farm	planet

33

Page 34

Classifying

Read the title of each book. Write the correct number in the ☐ to tell what kind of book each is.

1—Mystery   2—Sports   3—Science   4—Cooking
5—Riddles and Jokes   6—Famous People

Planets and Their Moons **3**
Baseball Greats **2**
A Laugh a Minute **5**
Great Pasta Dishes **4**
Young Abe Lincoln **6**
The Clue of the Broken Lock **1**
How to Collect Rocks **3**
Tennis Tips **2**

Read a sentence from each book. Write the number from each book on the correct line below.

4 Add two pounds of spaghetti to the boiling water and stir.
2 He was the only player to pitch a no-hitter in the 1969 World Series.
3 Several planets have at least three moons in their orbits.
6 Before he became president, he served as congressman.
5 Where does a five-hundred pound angry elephant sit?
3 Many rocks are used to tell how old the land is.
2 Each player needs a racket that is the correct size and weight.
1 She carefully examined the fingerprints on the trunk.

34

Page 35

Classifying

Is it fact or fantasy? Read each sentence. If the sentence tells a fact, circle the bee in the fact column. If the sentence is fantasy, circle the bee in the fantasy column.

"Bee"-lieve it or not!   Fact / Fantasy

1. Every year except leap year has 365 days.
2. Zebras' stripes can be washed off by rain.
3. Baseball and tennis are both sports.
4. December is the twelfth month of the year.
5. Some kinds of dogs can speak like people.
6. A supermarket sells many kinds of food.
7. Paul Bunyan carved the Grand Canyon.
8. The letters a, e, i, o and u are called vowels.
9. The moon is made of green cheese.
10. Beavers use their tails to help build their homes.

Write the correct letter from above on each line.

A queen bee flies only once in her lifetime!

35

Page 36

Classifying

Put a check in the box by the three words that go together. Underline the sentence which tells how they are alike.

☐ newspaper   ☑ hour
☑ minute   ☑ second
How are they alike?
They are about machines.
<u>They are about time.</u>

☑ heart   ☑ stomach
☑ brain   ☐ planet
How are they alike?
<u>They are about your body.</u>
They are about small things.

☑ Heading   ☐ pencil
☑ Greeting   ☑ Closing
How are they alike?
They are parts of a book.
<u>They are parts of a letter.</u>

☐ radio   ☑ piano
☑ trumpet   ☑ violin
How are they alike?
<u>They are musical instruments.</u>
They are made of wood.

Read the three words. Write a sentence which tells how they are alike.

1. knife   2. razor   3. scissors   How are they alike?
They all can cut.

1. Jupiter   2. Mars   3. Venus   How are they alike?
They are all planets.

1. Spring   2. Winter   3. Autumn   How are they alike?
They are all seasons.

36

Similarities and Differences (37)

Miss Freed says that watching TV and reading are alike because they are both entertainment. She says that watching TV is different from reading, though, because you choose what you are interested in from a list someone else makes. When you read, you can choose any subject you are interested in. Miss Freed says that reading makes you use your imagination and that people who read a lot learn more and read better.

Miss Freed asks the class to record the number of hours they watch TV each day for one week. Beth is shocked to see that she watches TV four hours each day. She decides to read more and watch TV less. She feels that she is getting smarter and smarter each day!

Unscramble and write.

Beth __records__ the time she watches TV each day for __one__ week.
rsdocre   one, two

Underline.

Reading and watching TV are both __transportation.__
__entertainment.__

Check.

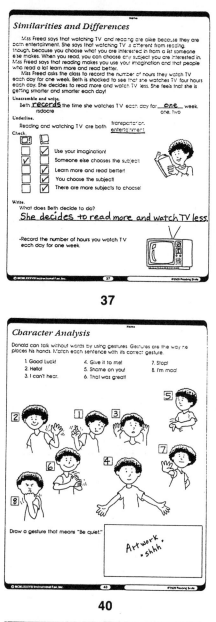

☑ Use your imagination!
☑ Someone else chooses the subject.
☐ Learn more and read better!
☑ You choose the subject!
☐ There are more subjects to choose!

Write.

What does Beth decide to do?
__She decides to read more and watch TV less.__

-Record the number of hours you watch TV each day for one week.

37

Similarities and Differences (38)

Donald invited six little elves for dinner last Thursday night. What a mess! They played jump rope with the spaghetti and swam in the clam chowder. They played catch with a pea and slid down the celery. At first, Donald was mad. Who likes to have their dinner guests playing with food? Do you?

When the elves saw that Donald was mad, they said they were sorry and would clean up the mess. "But you see," they explained, "we have a lot of imagination. To us, spaghetti is like a jump rope because it is so long and skinny. A bowl of soup is like a big swimming pool because it is liquid, or wet, and very warm, too. A pea is round like a ball and good for throwing. And the celery is smooth with nice edges for sliding."

"We always have lots of fun at dinner," they added.

The next time you have dinner, be careful. You never know what the little elves might be up to.

Circle yes or no.

The six little elves...

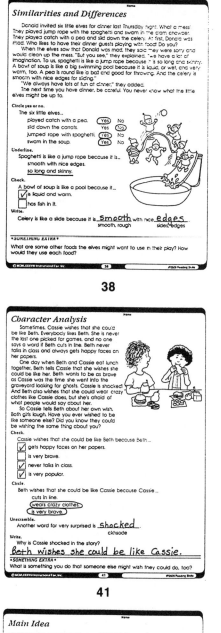

played catch with a pea   (Yes)   No
slid down the carrots   Yes   (No)
jumped rope with spaghetti   (Yes)   No
swam in the soup   (Yes)   No

Underline.

Spaghetti is like a jump rope because it is...
smooth with nice edges.
__so long and skinny.__

Check.

A bowl of soup is like a pool because it...
☑ is liquid and warm.
☐ has fish in it.

Write.

Celery is like a slide because it is __smooth__ with nice __edges.__
smooth, rough   sides/edges

SOMETHING EXTRA
What are some other foods the elves might want to use in their play? How would they use each food?

38

Similarities and Differences (39)

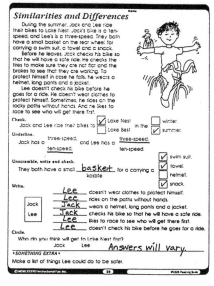

During the summer, Jack and Lee ride their bikes to Lake Nest. Jack's bike is a ten-speed, and Lee's is a three-speed. They both have a small basket on the rear wheel for carrying a swim suit, a towel and a snack. Before he leaves, Jack checks his bike so that he will have a safe ride. He checks the tires to make sure they are not flat and the brakes to see that they are working. To protect himself in case he falls, he wears a helmet, long pants and a jacket.

Lee doesn't check his bike before he goes for a ride. He doesn't wear clothes to protect himself. Sometimes, he rides on the rocky paths without hands. And he likes to race to see who will get there first.

Check.

Jack and Lee ride their bikes to   ☑ Lake Nest   in the   ☐ winter.
                                     ☐ Lake Best   ☑ summer.

Underline.

Jack has a   three-speed.   and Lee has a   __three-speed.__
              __ten-speed.__   ten-speed.

Unscramble, write and check.

They both have a small __basket__ for a carrying a
                        kasbte

☑ swim suit.
☑ towel.
☐ helmet.
☑ snack.

Write.

Jack	__Lee__	doesn't wear clothes to protect himself.
Lee	__Lee__	rides on the paths without hands.
	__Jack__	wears a helmet, long pants and a jacket.
	__Jack__	checks his bike so that he will have a safe ride.
	__Lee__	likes to race to see who will get there first.
	__Lee__	doesn't check his bike before he goes for a ride.

Circle.

Who do you think will get to Lake Nest first?
Jack   Lee   __Answers will vary.__

SOMETHING EXTRA
Make a list of things Lee could do to be safer.

39

Character Analysis (40)

Donald can talk without words by using gestures. Gestures are the way he places his hands. Match each sentence with its correct gesture.

1. Good Luck!   4. Give it to me!   7. Stop!
2. Hello!   5. Shame on you!   8. I'm mad!
3. I can't hear.   6. That was great!

Draw a gesture that means "Be quiet."

__Artwork. "shhh"__

40

Character Analysis (41)

Sometimes, Cassie wishes that she could be like Beth. Everybody likes Beth. She is never the last one picked for games, and no one says a word if Beth cuts in line. Beth never talks in class and always gets happy faces on her papers.

One day when Beth and Cassie eat lunch together, Beth tells Cassie that she wishes she could be like her. Beth wants to be as brave as Cassie was the time she went into the graveyard looking for ghosts. Cassie is shocked! And Beth also wishes that she could wear crazy clothes like Cassie does, but she's afraid of what people would say about her.

So Cassie tells Beth about her own wish. Both girls laugh. Have you ever wished to be like someone else? Did you know they could be wishing the same thing about you?

Check.

Cassie wishes that she could be like Beth because Beth...
☑ gets happy faces on her papers.
☐ is very brave.
☐ never talks in class.
☑ is very popular.

Circle.

Beth wishes that she could be like Cassie because Cassie...
cuts in line.
(wears crazy clothes.)
(is very brave.)

Unscramble.

Another word for very surprised is __shocked__
                                     ckhsode

Write.

Why is Cassie shocked in the story?
__Beth wishes she could be like Cassie.__

SOMETHING EXTRA
What is something you do that someone else might wish they could do, too?

41

Main Idea (42)

Read the messages. Write the correct letter by each main idea.

School Bulletin Board

A — Please sign up for a project to help get ready for our school carnival!

B — Cookie Sale Update Leading salesperson... so far is Lynn Davis!

C — ZOO DAY All third grade classes, March 26, leave at 9:00, back at 3:00. Bring lunch.

D — If you find a brown glove, see Mark in Mrs. King's 4th grade.

E — Anyone who is interested in joining the Art Club should see Ms. Hope after school.

F — 3rd and 4th grade band practice is now scheduled for next Thursday instead of this Thursday.

G — You Are Invited... to a going away party for Mr. Price Friday at 4:00 in the Gym.

(B) At this time, Lynn Davis has sold more cookies than anyone else.
(F) Third and fourth grade band practice has been postponed for a week.
(A) Students are encouraged to take part in the school carnival.
(D) Mark has lost one of his brown gloves.
(G) Everyone at school is invited to a going away party for Mr. Price.
(C) On March 26, the third graders will spend the day at the zoo.
(E) Ms. Hope is looking for new members for the Art Club.

42

Main Idea (43)

Unscramble each word. Circle the word which tells the main idea of each picture.

(daydream) lost   hunger   (learning)
tamdaaye   otls   unhreg   enrngig
5 2 8 1 7 4 3 6   4 2 1 3   2 3 1 5 4   2 5 4 7 8 1 6 3

(exercise) cloudy   whisper   (relax)
rieexcse   udcovl   rhiwesp   afxle
4 6 1 3 2 5 7 8   4 5 1 3 6 2   7 2 3 1 6 4 5   4 1 5 3 2

(delicious)   sleeping   (magical)
oledsiuei   iegsplde   gadicmi
7 3 5 1 9 4 8 2 6   6 4 8 1 5 2 7 3   3 2 6 7 5 1 4

huge
ghue
3 1 2 4

Now it's your turn!
Read each word and draw a matching picture for it.

| Artwork | Artwork | Artwork |
| sleepy | tiny | funny |

43

Main Idea (44)

Underline the correct sentence which tells the main idea of each picture.

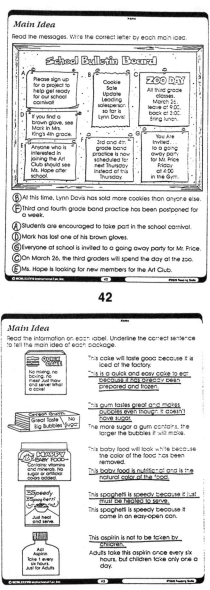

Thinking of nighttime makes me sleepy.
__I would love to be in the school play.__

__I can teach my brother to ride a bike.__
Bikes come in many different colors.

I wonder how much water is in the ocean.
__I hope I have fun at the beach.__

This birthday gift is very heavy.
__I can hardly wait for my birthday party.__

Look at each picture. Write a sentence which tells the main idea.

__Answers will vary.__

Main Idea:

Main Idea:

44

Main Idea (45)

Read the information on each label. Underline the correct sentence to tell the main idea of each package.

OUTTA SITE CAKE — No mixing, no baking, no mess! Just thaw and serve! What a cake!

This cake will taste good because it is iced at the factory.
__This is a quick and easy cake to eat because it has already been prepared and frozen.__

Great Gum — Great Taste — No Big Bubbles — No Sugar!

__This gum tastes great and makes bubbles even though it doesn't have sugar.__
The more sugar a gum contains, the larger the bubbles it will make.

HAPPY BABY FOOD — Contains: vitamins and minerals. No sugar or artificial colors added.

This baby food will look white because the color of the food has been removed.
__This baby food is nutritional and is the natural color of the food.__

Speedy Spaghetti! — Just heat and serve.

__This spaghetti is speedy because it just must be heated to serve.__
This spaghetti is speedy because it came in an easy-open can.

Act Aspirin — Take 1 every six hours. Just for Adults

__This aspirin is not to be taken by children.__
Adults take this aspirin once every six hours, but children take only one a day.

45

Page 46

Main Idea

Read the story that goes with each picture. Write the word which best describes each day on the line.

Some days
unlucky   hectic   special   relaxing   energetic

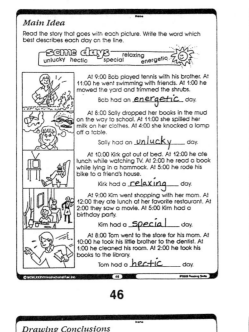

At 9:00 Bob played tennis with his brother. At 11:00 he went swimming with friends. At 1:00 he mowed the yard and trimmed the shrubs.

Bob had an **energetic** day.

At 8:00 Sally dropped her books in the mud on the way to school. At 11:00 she spilled her milk on her clothes. At 4:00 she knocked a lamp off a table.

Sally had an **unlucky** day.

At 10:00 Kirk got out of bed. At 12:00 he ate lunch while watching TV. At 2:00 he read a book while lying in a hammock. At 5:00 he rode his bike to a friend's house.

Kirk had a **relaxing** day.

At 9:00 Kim went shopping with her mom. At 12:00 they ate lunch at her favorite restaurant. At 2:00 they saw a movie. At 5:00 Kim had a birthday party.

Kim had a **special** day.

At 8:00 Tom went to the store for his mom. At 10:00 he took his little brother to the dentist. At 1:00 he cleaned his room. At 2:00 he took his books to the library.

Tom had a **hectic** day.

46

Page 47

Main Idea

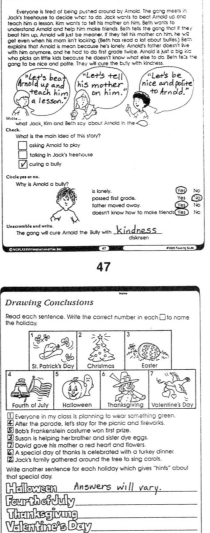

Everyone is tired of being pushed around by Arnold. The gang meets in Jack's treehouse to decide what to do. Jack wants to beat Arnold up and teach him a lesson. Kim wants to tell his mother on him. Beth wants to understand Arnold and help him make friends. Beth tells the gang that if they beat him up, Arnold will just be meaner. If they tell his mother on him, he will get even when his mom isn't looking. (Beth has read a lot about bullies.) Beth explains that Arnold is mean because he's lonely. Arnold's father doesn't live with him anymore, and he had to do first grade twice. Arnold is just a big kid who picks on little kids because he doesn't know what else to do. Beth tells the gang to be nice and polite. They will cure the bully with kindness.

"Let's beat Arnold up and teach him a lesson."   "Let's tell his mother on him."   "Let's be nice and polite to Arnold."

Write: what Jack, Kim and Beth say about Arnold in the ⬠

Check. What is the main idea of this story?
- [ ] asking Arnold to play
- [ ] talking in Jack's treehouse
- [x] curing a bully

Circle yes or no. Why is Arnold a bully?

is lonely.   **Yes**   No
passed first grade.   Yes   **No**
father moved away.   **Yes**   No
doesn't know how to make friends.   **Yes**   No

Unscramble and write.
The gang will cure Arnold the Bully with **kindness**
disknnen

47

Page 48

Drawing Conclusions

Look at each kind of clothing. Put a check by the two sentences which could explain why someone would wear the clothing. On the line, write another reason that someone would wear the clothing.

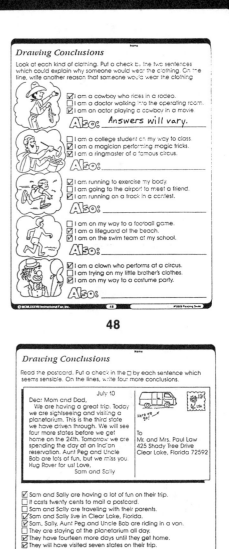

- [x] I am a cowboy who rides in a rodeo.
- [ ] I am a doctor walking into the operating room.
- [x] I am an actor playing a cowboy in a movie.

Also: Answers will vary.

- [ ] I am a college student on my way to class.
- [x] I am a magician performing magic tricks.
- [x] I am a ringmaster of a famous circus.

Also:

- [x] I am running to exercise my body.
- [ ] I am going to the airport to meet a friend.
- [x] I am running on a track in a contest.

Also:

- [ ] I am on my way to a football game.
- [x] I am a lifeguard at the beach.
- [x] I am on the swim team at my school.

Also:

- [x] I am a clown who performs at a circus.
- [ ] I am trying on my little brother's clothes.
- [x] I am on my way to a costume party.

Also:

48

Page 49

Drawing Conclusions

Look at the first picture. Put a check in the ☐ by each sentence which seems sensible. Look at the second picture. Write six sentences that tell your conclusions from the picture.

- [x] It is a very hot day.
- [x] The beach is a popular place to go.
- [ ] The beach is a quiet place to study.
- [x] Some people picnic at the beach.
- [x] A lifeguard helps protect swimmers.
- [x] It is hard to nap at a noisy beach.
- [ ] Sailing is just for kids.
- [x] Sailing and swimming are fun water sports.
- [x] Every town has a beach.

Write your own conclusions.
1. Answers will vary
2. _____
3. _____
4. _____
5. _____
6. _____

49

Page 50

Drawing Conclusions

Read each sentence. Write the correct number in each ☐ to name the holiday.

1 St. Patrick's Day	2 Christmas	3 Easter
4 Fourth of July	5 Halloween	6 Thanksgiving	7 Valentine's Day

- [1] Everyone in my class is planning to wear something green.
- [4] After the parade, let's stay for the picnic and fireworks.
- [5] Bob's Frankenstein costume won first prize.
- [3] Susan is helping her brother and sister dye eggs.
- [7] David gave his mother a red heart and flowers.
- [6] A special day of thanks is celebrated with a turkey dinner.
- [2] Jack's family gathered around the tree to sing carols.

Write another sentence for each holiday which gives "hints" about that special day.

Halloween Answers will vary.
Fourth of July _____
Thanksgiving _____
Valentine's Day _____
Easter _____

50

Page 51

Drawing Conclusions

Read the postcard. Put a check in the ☐ by each sentence which seems sensible. On the lines, write four more conclusions.

July 10
Dear Mom and Dad,
We are having a great trip. Today we are sightseeing and visiting a planetarium. This is the third state we have driven through. We will see four more states before we get home on the 24th. Tomorrow we are spending the day at an Indian reservation. Aunt Peg and Uncle Bob are lots of fun, but we miss you. Hug Rover for us! Love,
Sam and Sally

Here we go!

To
Mr. and Mrs. Paul Law
425 Shady Tree Drive
Clear Lake, Florida 72592

- [x] Sam and Sally are having a lot of fun on their trip.
- [ ] It costs twenty cents to mail a postcard.
- [ ] Sam and Sally are traveling with their parents.
- [x] Sam and Sally live in Clear Lake, Florida.
- [x] Sam, Sally, Aunt Peg and Uncle Bob are riding in a van.
- [ ] They are staying at the planetarium all day.
- [x] They have fourteen more days until they get home.
- [x] They will have visited seven states on their trip.

1. Answers will vary
2. _____
3. _____
4. _____

51

Page 52

Inference

Read the phrases on the left. Then choose an ending for each phrase from the list on the right. Write the letter of the ending in the blank space in the sentence. One is done for you.

1. If a joke is funny, **C**
2. If you water your plant, **H**
3. If the sun shines on the snow, **F**
4. If you leave your bike out in the rain, **A**
5. If you want to fly an airplane, **I**
6. If you want to cure your cold, **I**
7. If a lion is hungry, **J**
8. If you oversleep in the morning, **B**
9. If you ride a bike, **E**
10. If you get a new puppy, **G**

A. it will rust.
B. you will be late for school.
C. people will laugh.
D. you will have to take lessons.
E. you must follow the rules of the road.
F. it will melt.
G. you will want to give it a special name.
H. it will grow.
I. you will have to rest.
J. it will look for food.

52

Page 53

Inference

Cassie's mom is a carpenter. She likes to build nice houses for people to live in. She likes to work outside even when it is raining. When she was young like Cassie, she was good at building things like birdhouses and toy boxes. Her birdhouses and toy boxes were so good that she sold them at stores.

Kim's mom works in a store in Dukwilma Mall. She sells rugs and furniture. She likes helping people buy things to make their homes look nice. When she was young like Kim, she was good at selling things. She sold the most cookies for her Girl Scout Troop. She even sold five boxes to crabby Mr. Sorely who never left his house!

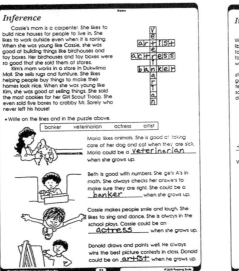

- Write on the lines in the puzzle above.

banker   veterinarian   actress   artist

Maria likes animals. She is good at taking care of her dog and cat when they are sick. Maria could be a **veterinarian** when she grows up.

Beth is good with numbers. She gets A's in math. She always checks her answers to make sure they are right. She could be a **banker** when she grows up.

Cassie makes people smile and laugh. She likes to sing and dance. She is always in the school plays. Cassie could be an **actress** when she grows up.

Donald draws and paints well. He always wins the best picture contests in class. Donald could be an **artist** when he grows up.

53

Page 54

Inference

Kim's dad is a librarian. He likes working inside where it is quiet and warm. When he was Kim's age, he helped the librarian Mrs. Sweetly in the school library. Mrs. Sweetly taught him much about how to be a good librarian. She told him that he would be a good librarian when he grew up. Kim's dad never forgot what Mrs. Sweetly said. He went to school to learn more about how to work in a library.

Beth's dad works for a newspaper. He's a newspaper reporter and writes stories about all the interesting and exciting things that happen in town. He likes going to different places and talking to people. When he said Beth's age, his teacher, Miss Gregory, helped him learn how to write. She said Beth's dad was so good at writing that he could get a job as a writer when he grew up. Beth's dad never forgot what Miss Gregory said.

teacher   scientist   photographer   mechanic

Write on the lines and in the pictures above.

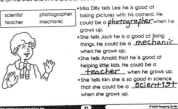

| scientist | photographer |
| teacher | mechanic |

- Miss Ditty tells Lee he is good at taking pictures with his camera. He could be a **photographer** when he grows up.
- She tells Jack he is a good at fixing things. He could be a **mechanic** when he grows up.
- She tells Arnold that he is good at helping little kids. He could be a **teacher** when he grows up.
- She tells Kim she is so good in science that she could be a **scientist** when she grows up.

54

IF0134

"I Love Reading"

Introducing our newest Homework Booklet series — **I Love Reading.** Each **I Love Reading** Homework Booklet contains 40 interesting stories and thorough comprehension activities.

IF0134 I Love Reading Level 3 Book 1

Stories about People and Places such as:
- What does a dairy farmer do?
- What is a lawyer?
- Who was Thomas Jefferson?
- What is a salary?
- What is rent?
- What is a bank?

Stories about Science and Nature such as:
- What is a weed?
- Why does a tree have bark?
- What is a crop?
- What are nuts?
- How is butter made?
- What is a satellite?

IF0135 I Love Reading Level 3 Book 2

Stories about People and Places such as:
- What is a neighborhood?
- What is a city?
- What is a plain?
- What is a map?
- What is a continent?
- What is the ocean?

Stories about Science and Nature such as:
- How does an elephant use its trunk?
- Why do zebras have stripes?
- Why don't ducks get wet when they swim?
- Why do bees buzz?
- What is a nerve?
- Why do your baby teeth come out?

IF0130 Mathematics Level 3

Practice with important math skills. Areas emphasized include: simple addition, addition with carrying, fractions, and decimals.

IF0132 Reading Skills Level 3

Enjoyable practice in developing reading skills. Highlighted areas include: fun with words, language tricks, using context clues, and other reading skills.

IF0131 Language Arts Level 3

Valuable practice in developing language arts skills. Areas emphasized include: consonant and vowel review, word wisdom, grammar, and other language skills.

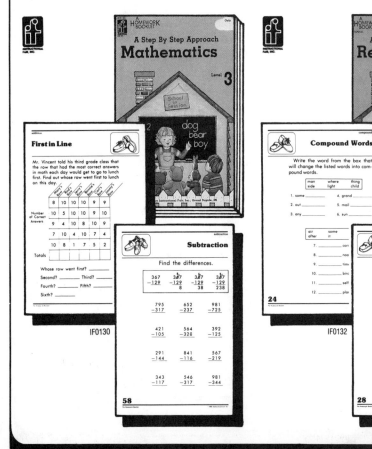

IF0130

IF0132

IF0131

Vocabulary

Read each sentence. Choose the correct word to complete each sentence. Color each puzzle space the correct color.

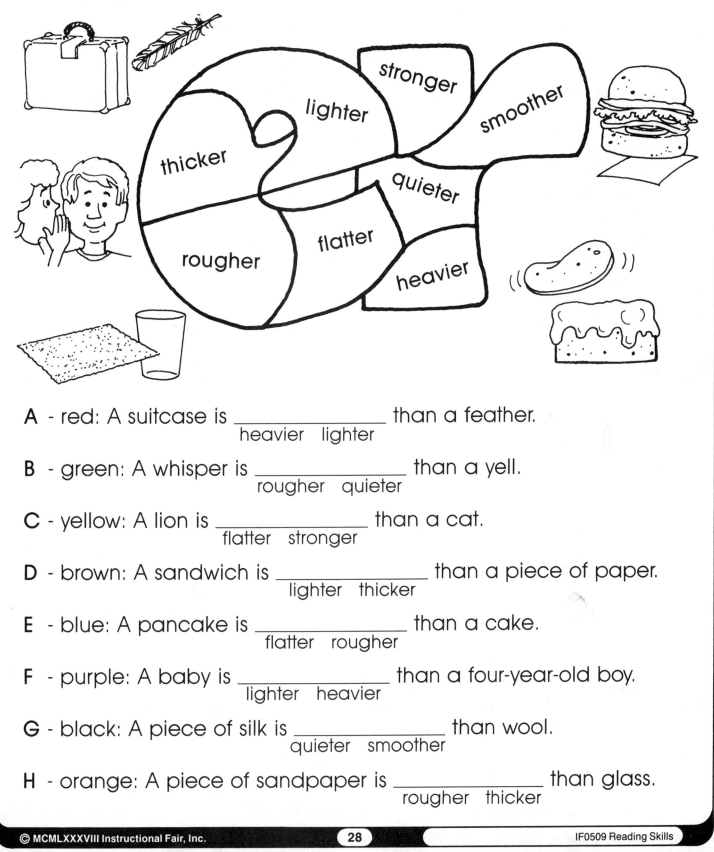

A - red: A suitcase is _____ than a feather.
    heavier   lighter

B - green: A whisper is _____ than a yell.
    rougher   quieter

C - yellow: A lion is _____ than a cat.
    flatter   stronger

D - brown: A sandwich is _____ than a piece of paper.
    lighter   thicker

E - blue: A pancake is _____ than a cake.
    flatter   rougher

F - purple: A baby is _____ than a four-year-old boy.
    lighter   heavier

G - black: A piece of silk is _____ than wool.
    quieter   smoother

H - orange: A piece of sandpaper is _____ than glass.
    rougher   thicker

Vocabulary

All around town are sights that you might see each day. But have you ever tried to describe them? Look at each picture. Think of four words to describe each picture. Write the words on the lines.

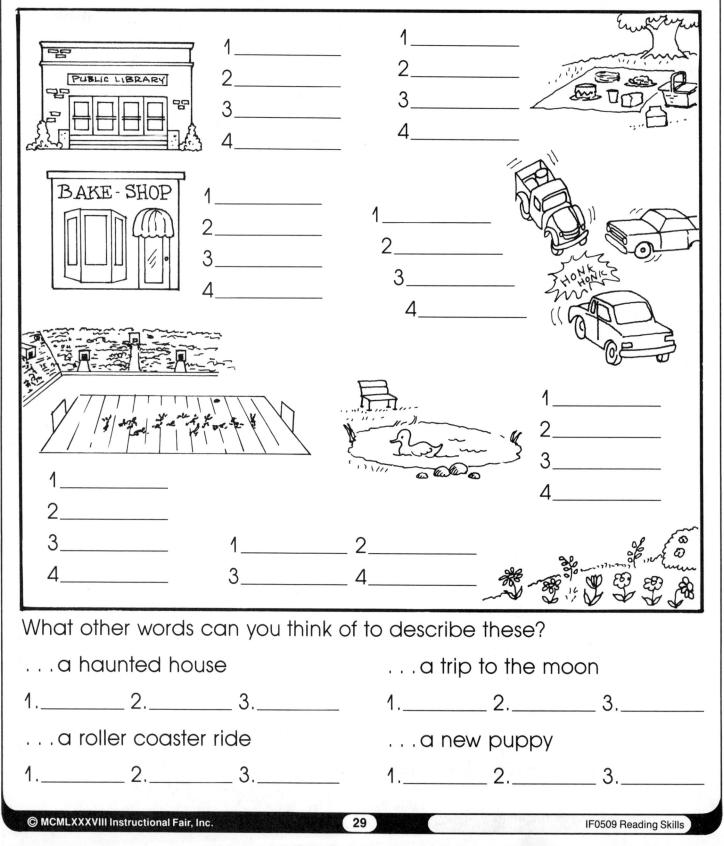

What other words can you think of to describe these?

. . .a haunted house

1._____ 2._____ 3._____

. . .a roller coaster ride

1._____ 2._____ 3._____

. . .a trip to the moon

1._____ 2._____ 3._____

. . .a new puppy

1._____ 2._____ 3._____

Vocabulary

Unscramble each word to complete the sentence. The first letter is circled. Color each space the correct color.

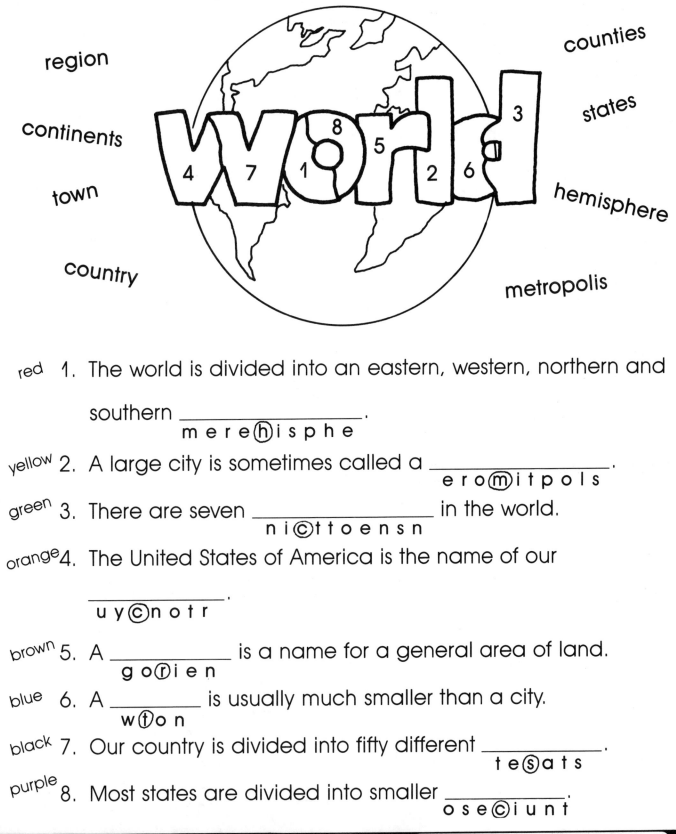

region

counties

continents

states

town

hemisphere

country

metropolis

red   1. The world is divided into an eastern, western, northern and

southern _____.
   m e r e (h) i s p h e

yellow   2. A large city is sometimes called a _____.
   e r o (m) i t p o l s

green   3. There are seven _____ in the world.
   n i (c) t t o e n s n

orange 4. The United States of America is the name of our

_____.
   u y (c) n o t r

brown 5. A _____ is a name for a general area of land.
   g o (r) i e n

blue   6. A _____ is usually much smaller than a city.
   w (t) o n

black 7. Our country is divided into fifty different _____.
   t e (s) a t s

purple 8. Most states are divided into smaller _____.
   o s e (c) i u n t

Classifying

1. Name 4 things that will:

float

1 _____ 2 _____

3 _____ 4 _____

2. Name 4 things that will:

rattle

1 _____ 2 _____

3 _____ 4 _____

3. Name 4 things that will:

roll

1 _____ 2 _____

3 _____ 4 _____

4. Name 4 things that will:

cut

1 _____ 2 _____

3 _____ 4 _____

5. Name 4 things that are:

sticky

1 _____ 2 _____

3 _____ 4 _____

6. Name 4 things that are:

smooth

1 _____ 2 _____

3 _____ 4 _____

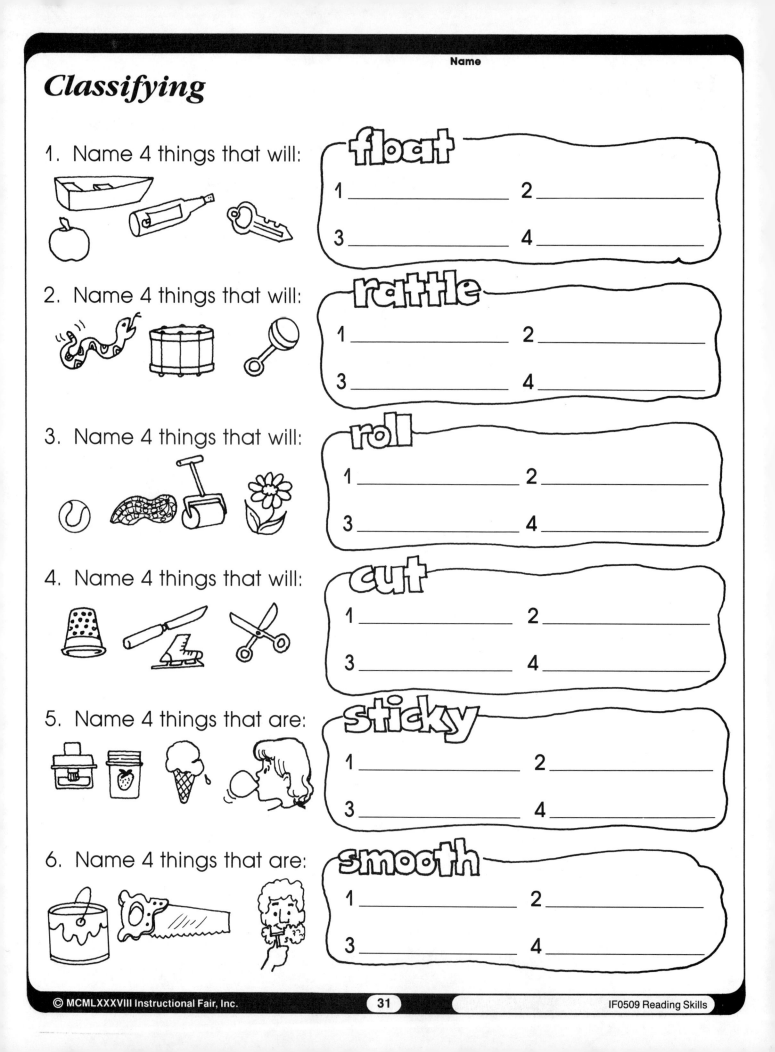

Classifying

Beth is going to the mountains on Friday, Saturday and Sunday. Her grandfather, aunt and cousin are going too. They will stay in Grandfather's cabin. When she is at the mountains, Beth will go skiing, sledding and ice skating. If it is too snowy, icy or windy, she will stay inside and read books, magazines or the newspaper. Beth is excited about her winter holiday.

Check.

Beth is going to the...

☐ beach.

☐ mountains.

Circle.

She feels...

brave.

excited.

Underline.

They will stay in Grandpa's...

motel.

lodge.

cabin.

Write.

Day Words	Family Words	Sports Words

Weather Words	Things to Read

Classifying

Write each word under its correct heading.
Check each word off as you write.

early	little	planet	huge	policeman
tiny	month	throw	fireman	beach
week	city	mailman	soon	eat
teacher	jump	late	library	skip
drive	baker	skinny	large	farm

Action Words	Job Words	Size Words

Time Words	Place Words	Write the place words in alphabetical order.

Classifying

Read the title of each book. Write the correct number in the ☐ to tell what kind of book each is.

1—Mystery   2—Sports   3—Science   4—Cooking
          5—Riddles and Jokes   6—Famous People

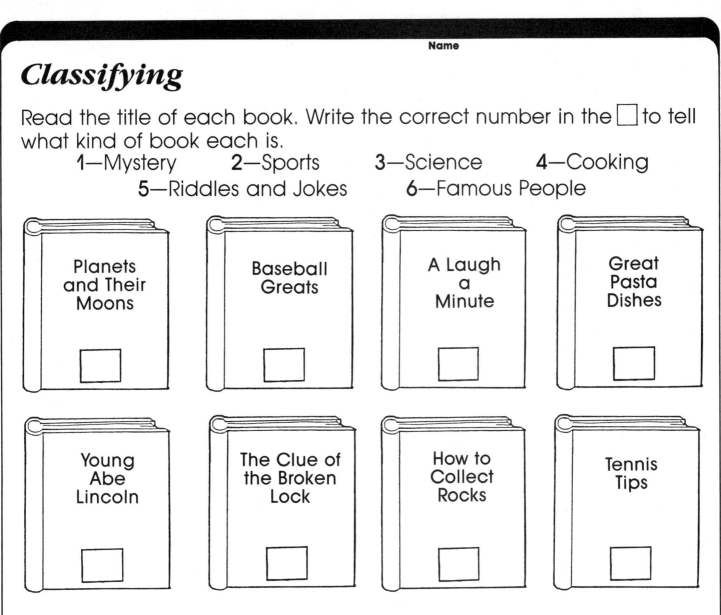

Read a sentence from each book. Write the number from each book on the correct line below.

___ Add two pounds of spaghetti to the boiling water and stir.

___ He was the only player to pitch a no-hitter in the 1969 World Series.

___ Several planets have at least three moons in their orbits.

___ Before he became president, he served as congressman.

___ Where does a five-hundred pound angry elephant sit?

___ Many rocks are used to tell how old the land is.

___ Each player needs a racket that is the correct size and weight.

___ She carefully examined the fingerprints on the trunk.

Classifying

Is it **fact** or **fantasy**? Read each sentence. If the sentence tells a fact, circle the bee in the fact column. If the sentence is fantasy, circle the bee in the fantasy column.

"Bee"-lieve it or not!

Fact   Fantasy

1. Every year except leap year has 365 days.   m   p
2. Zebras' stripes can be washed off by rain.   s   l
3. Baseball and tennis are both sports.   e   k
4. December is the twelfth month of the year.   o   b
5. Some kinds of dogs can speak like people.   b   y
6. A supermarket sells many kinds of food.   n   g
7. Paul Bunyan carved the Grand Canyon.   z   r
8. The letters a, e, i, o and u are called vowels.   u   w
9. The moon is made of green cheese.   a   i
10. Beavers use their tails to help build their homes.   f   h

Write the correct letter from above on each line.

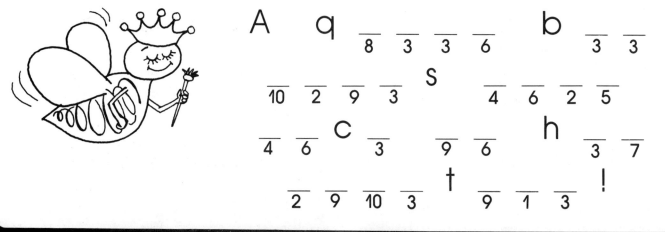

A   q _ _ _ _   b _ _
     8 3 3 6   3 3

     s
_ _ _ _   _ _ _ _
10 2 9 3   4 6 2 5

_ _ c _ _ _   h _ _
4 6 3 9 6   3 7

     t
_ _ _ _   _ _ _ !
2 9 10 3   9 1 3

Classifying

Put a check in the box by the three words that go together.
Underline the sentence which tells how they are alike.

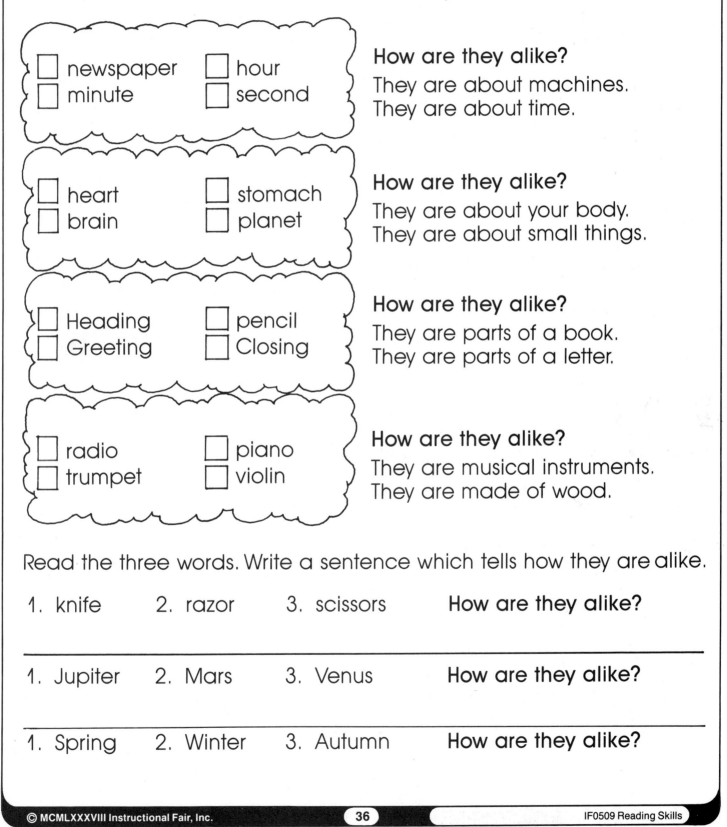

☐ newspaper   ☐ hour
☐ minute   ☐ second

How are they alike?
They are about machines.
They are about time.

☐ heart   ☐ stomach
☐ brain   ☐ planet

How are they alike?
They are about your body.
They are about small things.

☐ Heading   ☐ pencil
☐ Greeting   ☐ Closing

How are they alike?
They are parts of a book.
They are parts of a letter.

☐ radio   ☐ piano
☐ trumpet   ☐ violin

How are they alike?
They are musical instruments.
They are made of wood.

Read the three words. Write a sentence which tells how they are alike.

1. knife   2. razor   3. scissors   **How are they alike?**

_____

1. Jupiter   2. Mars   3. Venus   **How are they alike?**

_____

1. Spring   2. Winter   3. Autumn   **How are they alike?**

Similarities and Differences

Miss Freed says that watching TV and reading are alike because they are both entertainment. She says that watching TV is different from reading, though, because you choose what you are interested in from a list someone else makes. When you read, you can choose any subject you are interested in. Miss Freed says that reading makes you use your imagination and that people who read a lot learn more and read better.

Miss Freed asks the class to record the number of hours they watch TV each day for one week. Beth is shocked to see that she watches TV four hours each day. She decides to read more and watch TV less. She feels that she is getting smarter and smarter each day!

Unscramble and write.

Beth _____ the time she watches TV each day for _____ week.
　　　　rsdocre　　　　　　　　　　　　　　　　　　　　　　　　　one, two

Underline.

Reading and watching TV are both 　　transportation.
　　　　　　　　　　　　　　　　　　　　　entertainment.

Check.

☐　☐　　Use your imagination!

☐　☐　　Someone else chooses the subject!

☐　☐　　Learn more and read better!

☐　☐　　You choose the subject!

☐　☐　　There are more subjects to choose!

Write.

What does Beth decide to do?

_____

• Record the number of hours you watch TV each day for one week.

Similarities and Differences

Donald invited six little elves for dinner last Thursday night. What a mess! They played jump rope with the spaghetti and swam in the clam chowder. They played catch with a pea and slid down the celery. At first, Donald was mad. Who likes to have their dinner guests playing with food! Do you?

When the elves saw that Donald was mad, they said they were sorry and would clean up the mess. "But you see," they explained, "we have a lot of imagination. To us, spaghetti is like a jump rope because it is so long and skinny. A bowl of soup is like a big swimming pool because it is liquid, or wet, and very warm, too. A pea is round like a ball and good for throwing. And the celery is smooth with nice edges for sliding."

"We always have lots of fun at dinner," they added.

The next time you have dinner, be careful. You never know what the little elves might be up to.

Circle yes or no.

The six little elves...

played catch with a pea.	Yes	No
slid down the carrots.	Yes	No
jumped rope with spaghetti.	Yes	No
swam in the soup.	Yes	No

Underline.

Spaghetti is like a jump rope because it is...

    smooth with nice edges.

    so long and skinny.

Check.

A bowl of soup is like a pool because it...

☐ is liquid and warm.

☐ has fish in it.

Write.

Celery is like a slide because it is _____ with nice _____.

                                 smooth, rough   sides, edges

---

• SOMETHING EXTRA •

What are some other foods the elves might want to use in their play? How would they use each food?

Similarities and Differences

During the summer, Jack and Lee ride their bikes to Lake Nest. Jack's bike is a ten-speed, and Lee's is a three-speed. They both have a small basket on the rear wheel for carrying a swim suit, a towel and a snack.

Before he leaves, Jack checks his bike so that he will have a safe ride. He checks the tires to make sure they are not flat and the brakes to see that they are working. To protect himself in case he falls, he wears a helmet, long pants and a jacket.

Lee doesn't check his bike before he goes for a ride. He doesn't wear clothes to protect himself. Sometimes, he rides on the rocky paths without hands. And he likes to race to see who will get there first.

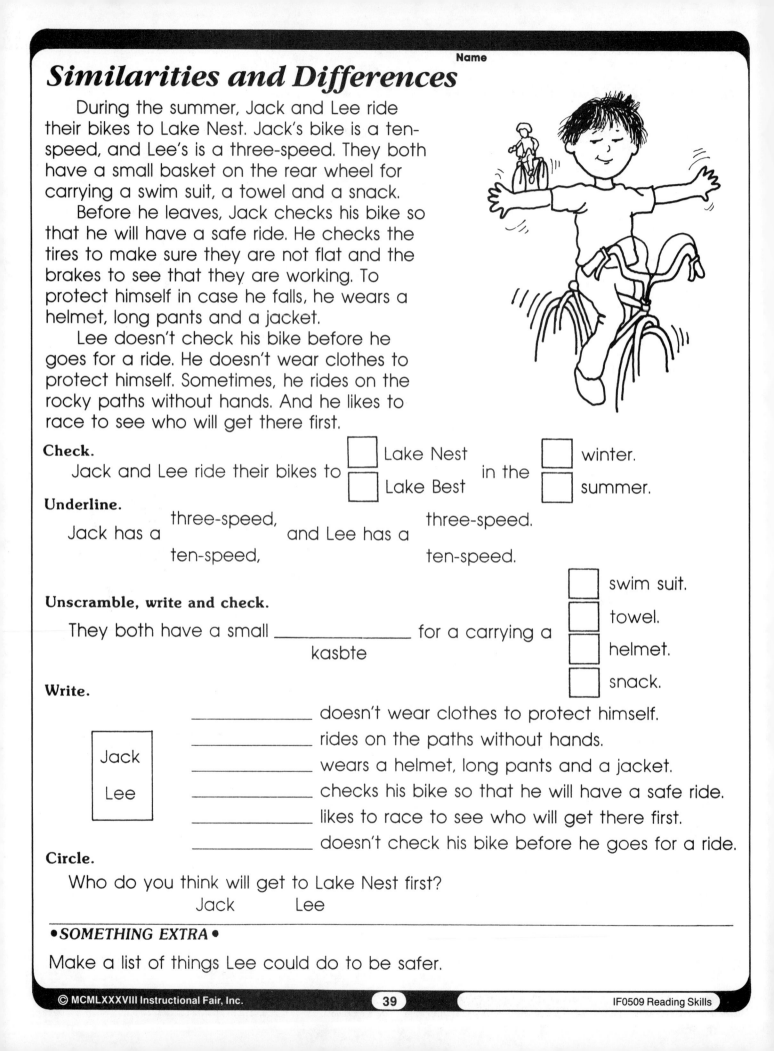

Check.
Jack and Lee ride their bikes to ☐ Lake Nest ☐ Lake Best in the ☐ winter. ☐ summer.

Underline.
Jack has a   three-speed,   and Lee has a   three-speed.
             ten-speed,   ten-speed.

Unscramble, write and check.
They both have a small _____ for a carrying a
                          kasbte

☐ swim suit.
☐ towel.
☐ helmet.
☐ snack.

Write.

Jack
Lee

_____ doesn't wear clothes to protect himself.
_____ rides on the paths without hands.
_____ wears a helmet, long pants and a jacket.
_____ checks his bike so that he will have a safe ride.
_____ likes to race to see who will get there first.
_____ doesn't check his bike before he goes for a ride.

Circle.
Who do you think will get to Lake Nest first?
            Jack   Lee

• **SOMETHING EXTRA** •

Make a list of things Lee could do to be safer.

Character Analysis

Donald can talk without words by using gestures. Gestures are the way he places his hands. Match each sentence with its correct gesture.

1. Good Luck!   4. Give it to me!   7. Stop!
2. Hello!   5. Shame on you!   8. I'm mad!
3. I can't hear.   6. That was great!

Draw a gesture that means "Be quiet."

Character Analysis

Sometimes, Cassie wishes that she could be like Beth. Everybody likes Beth. She is never the last one picked for games, and no one says a word if Beth cuts in line. Beth never talks in class and always gets happy faces on her papers.

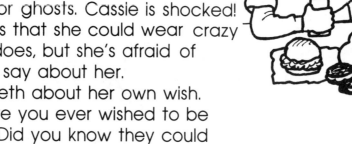

One day when Beth and Cassie eat lunch together, Beth tells Cassie that she wishes she could be like her. Beth wants to be as brave as Cassie was the time she went into the graveyard looking for ghosts. Cassie is shocked! And Beth also wishes that she could wear crazy clothes like Cassie does, but she's afraid of what people would say about her.

So Cassie tells Beth about her own wish. Both girls laugh. Have you ever wished to be like someone else? Did you know they could be wishing the same thing about you?

Check.

Cassie wishes that she could be like Beth because Beth...

☐ gets happy faces on her papers.

☐ is very brave.

☐ never talks in class.

☐ is very popular.

Circle.

Beth wishes that she could be like Cassie because Cassie...

cuts in line.

wears crazy clothes.

is very brave.

Unscramble.

Another word for very surprised is _____.

ckhsode

Write.

Why is Cassie shocked in the story?

_____

• *SOMETHING EXTRA* •

What is something you do that someone else might wish they could do, too?

Main Idea

Read the messages. Write the correct letter by each main idea.

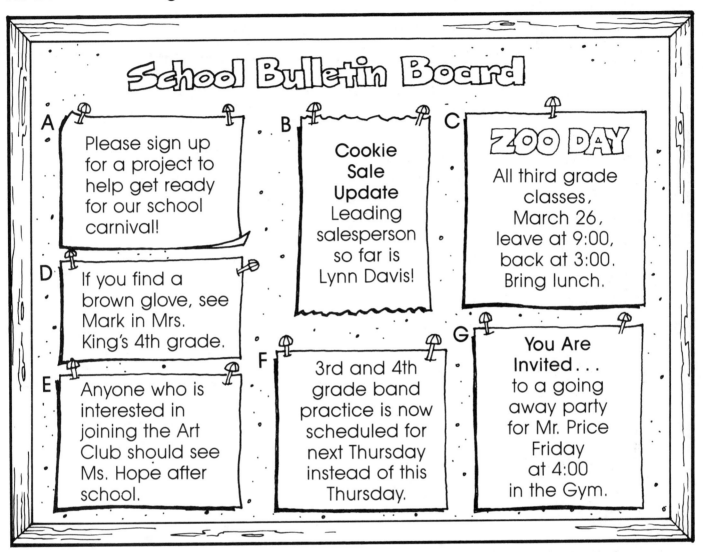

School Bulletin Board

A — Please sign up for a project to help get ready for our school carnival!

B — Cookie Sale Update Leading salesperson so far is Lynn Davis!

C — ZOO DAY All third grade classes, March 26, leave at 9:00, back at 3:00. Bring lunch.

D — If you find a brown glove, see Mark in Mrs. King's 4th grade.

E — Anyone who is interested in joining the Art Club should see Ms. Hope after school.

F — 3rd and 4th grade band practice is now scheduled for next Thursday instead of this Thursday.

G — You Are Invited... to a going away party for Mr. Price Friday at 4:00 in the Gym.

○ At this time, Lynn Davis has sold more cookies than anyone else.

○ Third and fourth grade band practice has been postponed for a week.

○ Students are encouraged to take part in the school carnival.

○ Mark has lost one of his brown gloves.

○ Everyone at school is invited to a going away party for Mr. Price.

○ On March 26, the third graders will spend the day at the zoo.

○ Ms. Hope is looking for new members for the Art Club.

Main Idea

Unscramble each word. Circle the word which tells the main idea of each picture.

r a m d a d y e
5 2 8 1 7 4 3 6

o t l s
2 4 1 3

u n h r e g
2 3 1 6 5 4

e n r n g l i a
2 5 4 7 8 1 6 3

r i e e x c s e
4 6 1 3 2 5 7 8

u d c o y l
4 5 1 3 6 2

r h i w e s p
7 2 3 1 6 4 5

a r x l e
4 1 5 3 2

o l c d s i u e i
7 3 5 1 9 4 8 2 6

g h u e
3 1 2 4

i e g s p l n e
6 4 8 1 5 2 7 3

g a a l c m i
3 2 6 7 5 1 4

Now it's your turn!
Read each word and draw a matching picture for it.

sleepy	tiny	funny

Main Idea

Underline the correct sentence which tells the main idea of each picture.

Thinking of nighttime makes me sleepy.

I would love to be in the school play.

I can teach my brother to ride a bike.

Bikes come in many different colors.

I wonder how much water is in the ocean.

I hope I have fun at the beach.

This birthday gift is very heavy.

I can hardly wait for my birthday party.

Look at each picture. Write a sentence which tells the main idea.

Main Idea: _____

_____

Main Idea: _____

_____

Main Idea

Read the information on each label. Underline the correct sentence to tell the main idea of each package.

This cake will taste good because it is iced at the factory.

This is a quick and easy cake to eat because it has already been prepared and frozen.

This gum tastes great and makes bubbles even though it doesn't have sugar.

The more sugar a gum contains, the larger the bubbles it will make.

This baby food will look white because the color of the food has been removed.

This baby food is nutritional and is the natural color of the food.

This spaghetti is speedy because it just must be heated to serve.

This spaghetti is speedy because it came in an easy-open can.

This aspirin is not to be taken by children.

Adults take this aspirin once every six hours, but children take only one a day.

Main Idea

Read the story that goes with each picture. Write the word which best describes each day on the line.

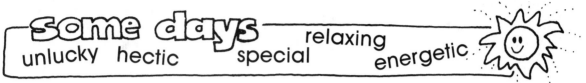

some days

unlucky   hectic   special   relaxing   energetic

At 9:00 Bob played tennis with his brother. At 11:00 he went swimming with friends. At 1:00 he mowed the yard and trimmed the shrubs.

Bob had an _____ day.

At 8:00 Sally dropped her books in the mud on the way to school. At 11:00 she spilled her milk on her clothes. At 4:00 she knocked a lamp off a table.

Sally had an _____ day.

At 10:00 Kirk got out of bed. At 12:00 he ate lunch while watching TV. At 2:00 he read a book while lying in a hammock. At 5:00 he rode his bike to a friend's house.

Kirk had a _____ day.

At 9:00 Kim went shopping with her mom. At 12:00 they ate lunch at her favorite restaurant. At 2:00 they saw a movie. At 5:00 Kim had a birthday party.

Kim had a _____ day.

At 8:00 Tom went to the store for his mom. At 10:00 he took his little brother to the dentist. At 1:00 he cleaned his room. At 2:00 he took his books to the library.

Tom had a _____ day.

Main Idea

Everyone is tired of being pushed around by Arnold. The gang meets in Jack's treehouse to decide what to do. Jack wants to beat Arnold up and teach him a lesson. Kim wants to tell his mother on him. Beth wants to understand Arnold and help him make friends. Beth tells the gang that if they beat him up, Arnold will just be meaner. If they tell his mother on him, he will get even when his mom isn't looking. (Beth has read a lot about bullies.) Beth explains that Arnold is mean because he's lonely. Arnold's father doesn't live with him anymore, and he had to do first grade twice. Arnold is just a big kid who picks on little kids because he doesn't know what else to do. Beth tells the gang to be nice and polite. They will cure the bully with kindness.

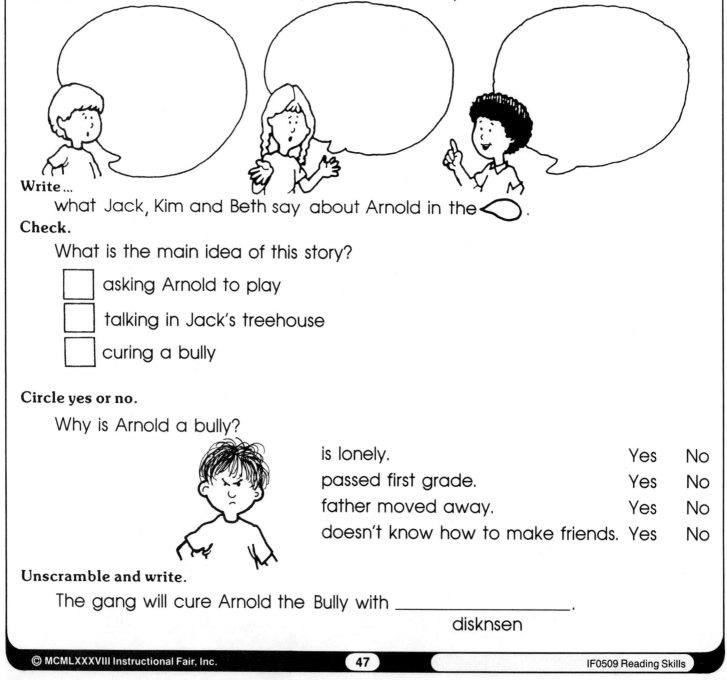

Write...

what Jack, Kim and Beth say about Arnold in the ◁◯.

Check.

What is the main idea of this story?

☐ asking Arnold to play

☐ talking in Jack's treehouse

☐ curing a bully

Circle yes or no.

Why is Arnold a bully?

is lonely.	Yes	No
passed first grade.	Yes	No
father moved away.	Yes	No
doesn't know how to make friends.	Yes	No

Unscramble and write.

The gang will cure Arnold the Bully with _____.

disknsen

Drawing Conclusions

Look at each kind of clothing. Put a check by the two sentences which could explain why someone would wear the clothing. On the line, write another reason that someone would wear the clothing.

☐ I am a cowboy who rides in a rodeo.
☐ I am a doctor walking into the operating room.
☐ I am an actor playing a cowboy in a movie.
Also: _____

☐ I am a college student on my way to class.
☐ I am a magician performing magic tricks.
☐ I am a ringmaster of a famous circus.
Also: _____

☐ I am running to exercise my body.
☐ I am going to the airport to meet a friend.
☐ I am running on a track in a contest.
Also: _____

☐ I am on my way to a football game.
☐ I am a lifeguard at the beach.
☐ I am on the swim team at my school.
Also: _____

☐ I am a clown who performs at a circus.
☐ I am trying on my little brother's clothes.
☐ I am on my way to a costume party.
Also: _____

IF0509 Reading Skills

Drawing Conclusions

Look at the first picture. Put a check in the ☐ by each sentence which seems sensible. Look at the second picture. Write six sentences that tell your conclusions from the picture.

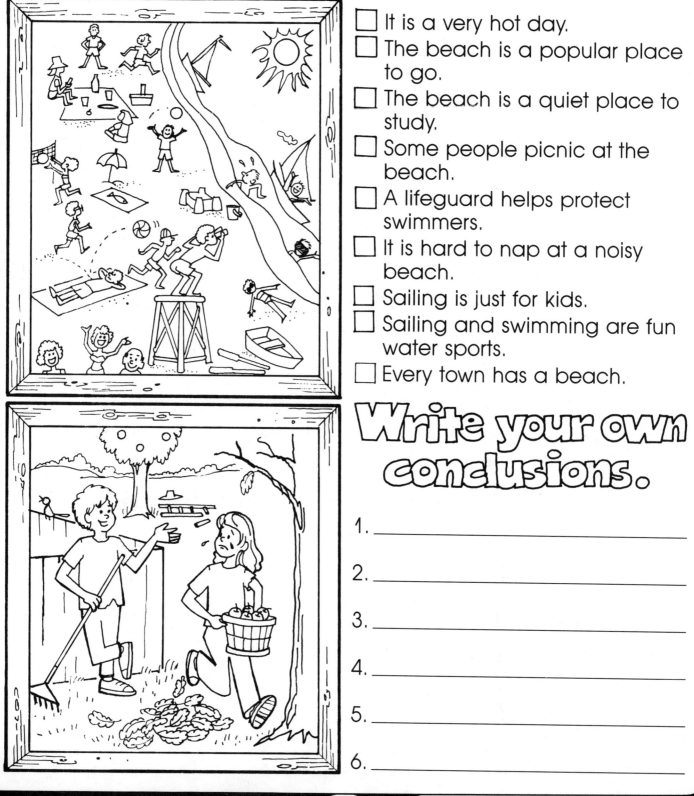

☐ It is a very hot day.
☐ The beach is a popular place to go.
☐ The beach is a quiet place to study.
☐ Some people picnic at the beach.
☐ A lifeguard helps protect swimmers.
☐ It is hard to nap at a noisy beach.
☐ Sailing is just for kids.
☐ Sailing and swimming are fun water sports.
☐ Every town has a beach.

Write your own conclusions.

1. _____

2. _____

3. _____

4. _____

5. _____

6. _____

Drawing Conclusions

Read each sentence. Write the correct number in each ☐ to name the holiday.

1 St. Patrick's Day	2 Christmas	3 Easter
4 Fourth of July	5 Halloween	6 Thanksgiving	7 Valentine's Day

☐ Everyone in my class is planning to wear something green.
☐ After the parade, let's stay for the picnic and fireworks.
☐ Bob's Frankenstein costume won first prize.
☐ Susan is helping her brother and sister dye eggs.
☐ David gave his mother a red heart and flowers.
☐ A special day of thanks is celebrated with a turkey dinner.
☐ Jack's family gathered around the tree to sing carols.

Write another sentence for each holiday which gives "hints" about that special day.

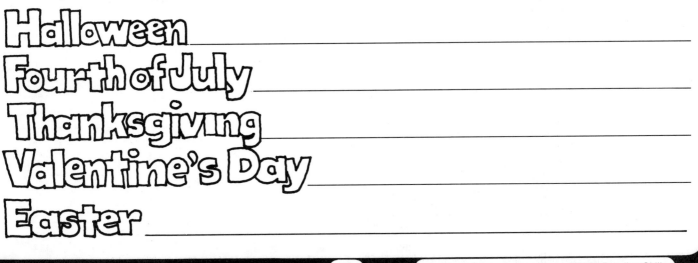

Halloween _____

Fourth of July _____

Thanksgiving _____

Valentine's Day _____

Easter _____

Drawing Conclusions

Read the postcard. Put a check in the □ by each sentence which seems sensible. On the lines, write four more conclusions.

July 10

Dear Mom and Dad,
  We are having a great trip. Today we are sightseeing and visiting a planetarium. This is the third state we have driven through. We will see four more states before we get home on the 24th. Tomorrow we are spending the day at an Indian reservation. Aunt Peg and Uncle Bob are lots of fun, but we miss you. Hug Rover for us! Love,
                Sam and Sally

Here we go!

To
Mr. and Mrs. Paul Law
425 Shady Tree Drive
Clear Lake, Florida 72592

□ Sam and Sally are having a lot of fun on their trip.
□ It costs twenty cents to mail a postcard.
□ Sam and Sally are traveling with their parents.
□ Sam and Sally live in Clear Lake, Florida.
□ Sam, Sally, Aunt Peg and Uncle Bob are riding in a van.
□ They are staying at the planetarium all day.
□ They have fourteen more days until they get home.
□ They will have visited seven states on their trip.

1 _____
2 _____
3 _____
4 _____

Inference

Read the phrases on the left. Then choose an ending for each phrase from the list on the right. Write the letter of the ending in the blank space in the sentence. One is done for you.

1. If a joke is funny, ___C___ .

2. If you water your plant, _____ .

3. If the sun shines on the snow, _____ .

4. If you leave your bike out in the rain, _____ .

5. If you want to fly an airplane, _____ .

6. If you want to cure your cold, _____ .

7. If a lion is hungry, _____ .

8. If you oversleep in the morning, _____ .

9. If you ride a bike, _____ .

10. If you get a new puppy, _____ .

A. it will rust.

B. you will be late for school.

C. people will laugh.

D. you will have to take lessons.

E. you must follow the rules of the road.

F. it will melt.

G. you will want to give it a special name.

H. it will grow.

I. you will have to rest.

J. it will look for food.

Inference

Cassie's mom is a carpenter. She likes to build nice houses for people to live in. She likes to work outside even when it is raining. When she was young like Cassie, she was good at building things like birdhouses and toy boxes. Her birdhouses and toy boxes were so good that she sold them at stores.

Kim's mom works in a store in Dukwilma Mall. She sells rugs and furniture. She likes helping people buy things to make their homes look nice. When she was young like Kim, she was good at selling things. She sold the most cookies for her Girl Scout Troop. She even sold five boxes to crabby Mr. Sorely who never left his house!

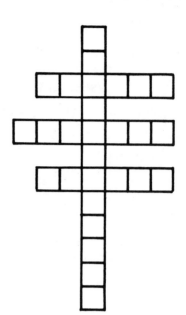

• Write on the lines and in the puzzle above.

banker	veterinarian	actress	artist

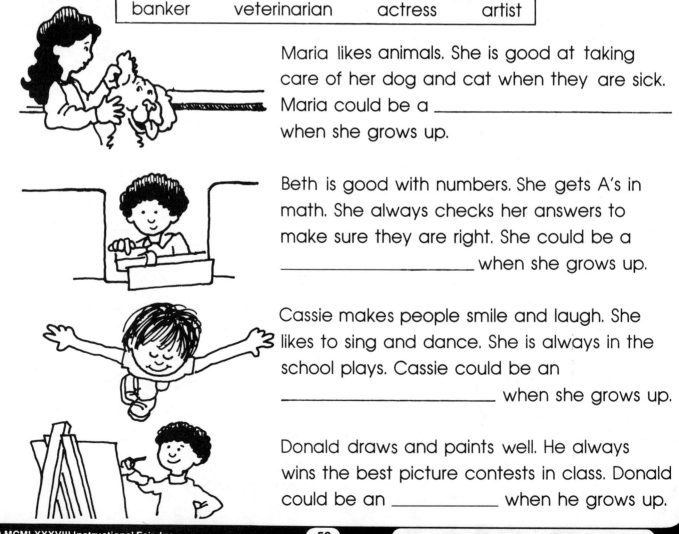

Maria likes animals. She is good at taking care of her dog and cat when they are sick. Maria could be a _____ when she grows up.

Beth is good with numbers. She gets A's in math. She always checks her answers to make sure they are right. She could be a _____ when she grows up.

Cassie makes people smile and laugh. She likes to sing and dance. She is always in the school plays. Cassie could be an _____ when she grows up.

Donald draws and paints well. He always wins the best picture contests in class. Donald could be an _____ when he grows up.

       IF0509 Reading Skills

Inference

Kim's dad is a librarian. He likes working inside where it is quiet and warm. When he was Kim's age, he helped the librarian Mrs. Sweetly in the school library. Mrs. Sweetly taught him much about how to be a good librarian. She told him that he would be a good librarian when he grew up. Kim's dad never forgot what Mrs. Sweetly said. He went to school to learn more about how to work in a library.

Beth's dad works for a newspaper. He's a newspaper reporter and writes stories about all the interesting and exciting things that happen in town. He likes going to different places and talking to people. When he was Beth's age, his teacher, Miss Gregory, helped him learn how to write. She said Beth's dad was so good at writing that he could get a job as a writer when he grew up. Beth's dad never forgot what Miss Gregory said.

_____ _____ _____ _____

Write on the lines and in the pictures above.

scientist	photographer
teacher	mechanic

- Miss Dilly tells Lee he is good at taking pictures with his camera. He could be a _____ when he grows up.

- She tells Jack he is a good at fixing things. He could be a _____ when he grows up.

- She tells Arnold that he is good at helping little kids. He could be a _____ when he grows up.

- She tells Kim she is so good in science that she could be a _____ when she grows up.

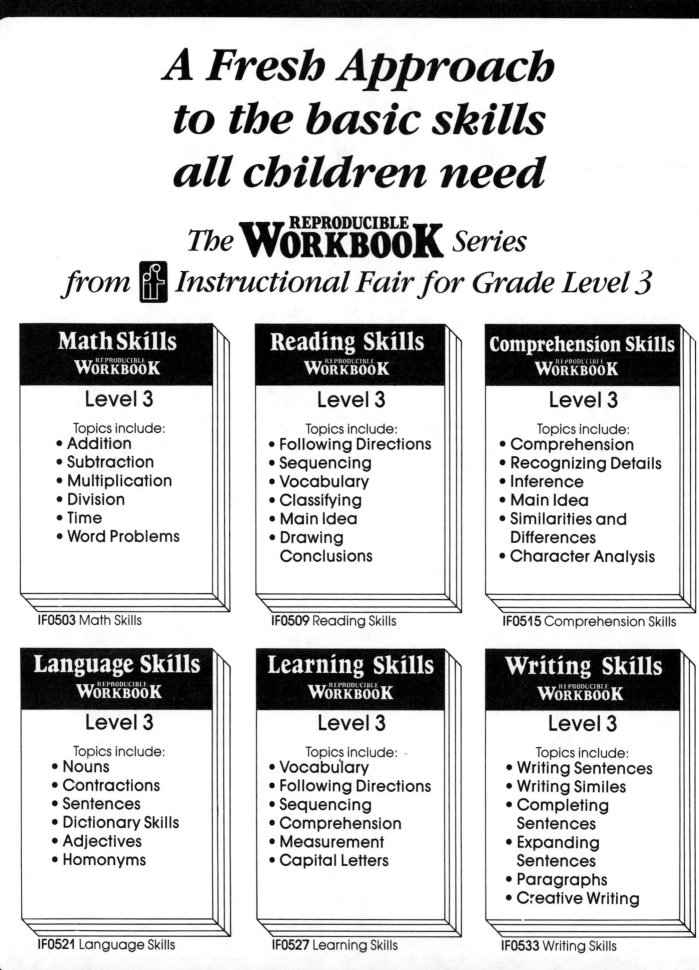

A Fresh Approach to the basic skills all children need

The REPRODUCIBLE WORKBOOK Series

from Instructional Fair for Grade Level 3

Math Skills
REPRODUCIBLE WORKBOOK
Level 3

Topics include:
- Addition
- Subtraction
- Multiplication
- Division
- Time
- Word Problems

IF0503 Math Skills

Reading Skills
REPRODUCIBLE WORKBOOK
Level 3

Topics include:
- Following Directions
- Sequencing
- Vocabulary
- Classifying
- Main Idea
- Drawing Conclusions

IF0509 Reading Skills

Comprehension Skills
REPRODUCIBLE WORKBOOK
Level 3

Topics include:
- Comprehension
- Recognizing Details
- Inference
- Main Idea
- Similarities and Differences
- Character Analysis

IF0515 Comprehension Skills

Language Skills
REPRODUCIBLE WORKBOOK
Level 3

Topics include:
- Nouns
- Contractions
- Sentences
- Dictionary Skills
- Adjectives
- Homonyms

IF0521 Language Skills

Learning Skills
REPRODUCIBLE WORKBOOK
Level 3

Topics include:
- Vocabulary
- Following Directions
- Sequencing
- Comprehension
- Measurement
- Capital Letters

IF0527 Learning Skills

Writing Skills
REPRODUCIBLE WORKBOOK
Level 3

Topics include:
- Writing Sentences
- Writing Similes
- Completing Sentences
- Expanding Sentences
- Paragraphs
- Creative Writing

IF0533 Writing Skills
